VINTAGE WRITING INSTRUCTION

Vintage Writing Instruction

Edited by Bryce Beattie

Articles by Leigh Brackett, Lester Dent, Robert Leslie Bellem, John Gallishaw, Laurence D'Orsay, Culpeper Chunn, Lurton Blassingame, Ward Macauley, Richard Darnell, Sara H. Sterling, Glenn H. Harris, Barry Scobee, Herbert C McKay, Thomas H. Uzzell, Archie Joscelyn, Harry Stephen Keeler, Roxanne Barber Rogers, Oliver Poole, Clarke Venable, Bessie White Smith, Leon Mones, Frank H. Williams, Sonya Levien, Magda Leigh, Frank Bennett

Published by Baby Katie Media, LLC

Table of Contents

Introduction..5

Why Stories are Rejected.................................6

From an Editor's Note-book............................9

A Word About Setting....................................13

Where to Get Your Ideas for Plots................15

What is Interest?..17

Are You Working or Wishing?......................20

Should You Write Pot Boilers?......................24

How to Make a Story Interesting..................31

Drama in the Short Story..............................54

The Science Fiction Field..............................72

Break it Up!..85

Plausibility is a Sometime Thing..................91

Hand Me That Scalpel, Nurse......................97

Wave Those Tags..100

"E" Plus Motion..109

A Method for Analyzing the Short Story.....114

Are You a Good Salesman?...........................120

Characterization...125

Cinematic Values in Story Writing..............132

Horror in the Ghost Story............................138

How to Create Plots......................................141

Produce-and Think!......................................152

Restraint-a Dangerous Virtue......................156

The Angle of Narration.................................166

Why I Decline Stories...................................173

How to Write Description Without Slowing the Story.....183

The Poorest Excuse.......................................188

Thank You for Reading.................................191

INTRODUCTION

Over the years, I've collected a large pile of old writing instruction. Crumbling magazines, yellowed books, and scans of both have place on my shelf and hard drives. I love it, and I'm constantly surprised the useful gems of writing instruction I find inside. And don't get me wrong, I'm not saying that all old advice is good just because it is old. Some of it is fluff. Some of it is quite dated. Some of it is advice that everybody has heard a million times, but still almost nobody follows. A lot of it is useful, however, and just as valuable today as when it was written.

I've scanned, corrected, read, and corrected some more a sea of writing articles from these old sources. It has been a great deal like when I am reading the slush pile for the magazine I publish. I've learned a great deal and I hope the work has made me a better writer and editor.

That said, I don't want to be your writing guru. I don't want to sell you a subscription to my secret author's mentoring club. I have no interest in establishing a brand for myself as the "master tutor of fictioneering" or anything like that.

All I want is to share some of the great old writing advice that has come my way. And I'm pretty excited to share some of these. There is a retro-hugo-winning article by Leigh Brackett. Prolific pulpateers Lester Dent and Robert Leslie Bellem have bits. And "How to Make a Story Interesting" is one of the best works on the craft of writing I have ever read. There are practical techniques, as well as reminders to a proper writing mindset. A little bit of everything.

So here I am, publishing a second book of reprints. If you liked *Pulp Era Writing Tips*, I hope you'll enjoy this one even more.

Hopefully, you will find the articles herein useful in your writing journey, too.

Why Stories are Rejected

By Ward Macauley
Originally published in the April 1903 issue of *The Editor*
Reader for "Wayside Tales."

I have read a great deal lately, in the way of complaint, that "readers" do not give writers sufficient consideration. It may not be amiss to say that the shoe is sometimes on the other foot. I can vouch for it, that writers very often submit manuscripts which, from a mechanical standpoint, show that the feelings of the reader have not been considered in the least. Nor is the sensitive reader offended only by the preparation of the manuscript; too often the story is so hopeless as too create disgust.

I suppose the most helpful things I can tell you are some of the reasons why a story is, or is not, available for publication in a fiction magazine of the type of "Wayside Tales."

In the first place, as a hint, let me say: Write an exceedingly brief note to accompany your manuscript. Indeed, unless you have something special to say, I see no need of any communication. Simply be sure that your name and address is in the corner of the first page. What you write in a letter, remember, makes positively no difference; it is what you write in the story that counts. So I advise you to expend your surplus energy there.

A typewritten manuscript is, other things being equal, much more likely to be accepted than a pen written one. In the first place, nearly all absolutely hopeless stories are in handwriting. It is the trademark of the novice. The officeboys, the butchers, and the others who think they can write a story, send it written in ink or even with a pencil. A typewritten manuscript, therefore, is usually recognized as being at least worth a careful consideration. It certainly receives more prompt attention. I know that, because human weakness cannot but defer reading villainous writing as long as possible. I must say, however, that I prefer good, plain handwriting to some of the wretched type copies we receive. Dim, blurred, full of errors, many of them are certainly a test to our patience. To be typewritten, therefore, is not enough. A manuscript should be typewritten well.

Attempted fine writing, I think, is on the whole the most general cause of rejection. High-flown, flowery language brings a smile to the reader's face and an "N. G. Reject" to the remark column of the report on the manuscript. Don't do it; that is all I can say. I find that many otherwise good stories are marred, spoiled and eternally condemned by a ridiculous use of poetic terms.

Unnatural dialogue is another cardinal sin of the average writer. Please remember that a man seldom, if ever, says, "horrid," "lovely," "delightful," etc., and that if you want your story to please you must not put such words in the mouths of your male characters. The other day, as an instance of this error, I read an excellent story, that was marred by this sentence, supposed to be used by a cowboy: "See those gesticulating men." Did anyone, out on the plains, ever utter such a sentence in real life?

There is also the common error of using obsolete or unknown words. This makes the conversation stilted, and the characters puppets, instead of real men and women.

Rank improbability is another fault that puts many stories out of the running. Don't have the eternal laws of gravitation suspended to meet the exigencies of your plot.

Trite plots are a very effective means of making stories unavailable. For example, never write a story in which a man makes love to a girl and then discovers that she is engaged to another. That is so very old, and has been used so much, that one pauses to wonder why any author should be foolish enough to think that a reader could be surprised at the climax. Unless your story has something original, either in matter or manner, your chances have gone a-glimmering.

The other day I received a story, accompanied by a letter in which the author said : "I do not know what kind of an ending you prefer, so I send two. You can take your choice." What do you think of that? If an author cannot make up his mind how to end his story, how can he expect an editor to? A story with two endings is no story at all, and, indeed, the one in question was not much of a tale and riot acceptable with either ending.

Many so-called stories I read are not, in fact, stories at all. They are essays, descriptive articles, religious exortations,—what you will; but they are not stories.

I believe that the best stories are the ones that portray an attractive and inspiring phase of real life. The best story I have ever been given to read was a tale of a southern minster, who delivered an address, arraigning politicians, before a political convention. He was, at once, nominated for sheriff. The story of how he carried his ideals into real life was immensely interesting, and the character work of a rare order. So I say, the most acceptable stories are lifelike, rather than bizarre, or fantastic. The average reader will care more for a well-told story like the one I have outlined, than he will for some unbelievable tale of gems of fabulous worth, or other chronicles of that ilk.

Most of all, have your stories in a presentable shape. Put yourself in the place of the reader; then you will think twice before you send him a scrawl.

Lastly, let me say that we receive more good, really good, available stories than we can possibly use; so I can vouch for it that a "rejection is no reflection on the merit of the manuscripts."

Some of the dated advice here is easily updated. When he speaks of sending in typewritten stories, just think "follow formatting guidelines."

I have never received a submission asking me to choose the ending, but Macauley's other warnings are skills with which many writers still struggle. And, I always have a similar problem as the one he lastly describes-there are always more publishable submissions than I have space for.

From an Editor's Note-book

By Richard Darnell
Originally published in the March 1925 issue of *Writer's Digest*

Some of my correspondents apparently have an idea that the chief aim in life of many editors is to discourage the beginning writer; consequently it gives me great pleasure to quote from a letter just now on my desk: "I have met with nothing but help and interest from every editor, and if I fail I feel that it is entirely my fault in being unable to produce good stuff." Now there is the right spirit. Editors do want writers to succeed. They welcome the new writer to the fold.

In this connection I think I am revealing no secret if I say that Mr. Hoffman, of Adventure, is one who takes particular pains to make the new writer feel that he is welcome. When accepting a manuscript he sends a letter of appreciation. As soon as possible he advises the writer the issue of the magazine in which his story will appear. He asks for personal data for the purpose of giving him some publicity in their page devoted to contributors. He gives him the opportunity of copyrighting his story in his own name if desired, and instructs him how to reserve second serial rights and how best to make same profitable.

In their "clip sheet" sent out to newspapers and magazines Adventure endeavors always to bring the name of the author to the front, and not to keep all the publicity for the magazine and the editor.

Yes, the editor is the best friend a young writer can have. Never mistake the truth of this assertion.

~

In every mining center will be found an assay office with an official in charge whose duty it is to test and report upon all specimens of ore that may be submitted to him. Prospectors searching for "color," for "pay-ore," and thinking that they have found it, eagerly bring thither their treasure-trove and anxiously await the verdict as to whether it is gold or dross.

The chemist in his laboratory analyzes the leaf, the shrub, or the flower to find if it contains aught of good or evil for the help or harm of man.

Unfortunately there are no assay offices or chemical laboratories for the writer in which he may have tested the creations of his brain, to discover if they are good or bad, false or true. If there were such, much trouble might be saved both to writers and editors.

But in the absence of such help every writer should learn to be his own assayer, his own analytical chemist.

A generation ago John Habberton became famous through his "Helen's Babies." These diverting youngsters were always interested to see the wheels go round, and a clock or a watch was of no interest to them except to be pulled apart to discover what made it go.

Now I wonder if it ever has occurred to you to analyze any published story that came under your observation? To take it apart, to discover its springs of action, how put together, the things in it that made it go? If any of you have not yet done this, it is time to begin. Take a story, any story, front any current magazine, study it to find the points of interest, examine it as to siting and atmosphere, ascertain if the characters impress you as real individuals, if the incidents contain anything of interest, if the situations are natural or forced. Is there a quality of suspense which makes you anxious to discover the end, and the solution of the problem which constitutes the plot? Are your sympathies enlisted for one or the other of the characters? Is there a quality of humor? Is there an emotional element that causes your pulses to quicken?

In the answer to these questions will be found much that will enable you to test your own story, for you will have found what makes the wheels go round, and thus you should be able to apply the mechanism to your own work.

~

From time to time the Writer's Digest has had much to say about hackneyed story themes, calling attention of writers to various types of these specifically. The one which perhaps most often has been referred to is that of little domestic infelicities, often centering about money questions.

Now comes the People's Popular Monthly, Des Moines, Ia., and says they are receiving a rather constant deluge of stories telling about wives who have a hard time getting money from their husbands. Needless to say, these are not the sort that draw checks from the editor of that magazine. If you can't help writing such, all right, go ahead and do it for your own satisfaction, but don't bother editors with them.

~

In a review before me of a collection of short stories, the truism is uttered that there are, after all, only two main varieties of the short story, the printable and the unprintable.

It writers will seriously study this assertion it may help them solve that ever-recurring question "Why are some stories accepted and others returned?" It is because, in the eyes of the editors, some are printable and some are not printable. By this I do not mean that in the latter is anything so objectionable that it should not be displayed on the printed page, but merely that it is not printable in that particular magazine and from that particular editor's viewpoint.

This assertion may still be further emphasized by the statement recently made by a publisher (who has a list of several popular magazines) that within eight months past his office has received and examined approximately 46,000 manuscripts.

It doesn't require a mathematician to figure out that the great majority were necessarily returned to writers; but — if the writers had taken care to give that editor something new, something directly in line with his publication, and something developed with literary skill he would have stood a better chance to be among the accepted minority than with the rejected majority.

And there is one point in the above worthy of particular consideration — that is, that a writer should familiarize himself with the publication to which he is offering his material. Styles in literature change. New publications are appearing almost daily and each one has a definite object, purposes to offer to the public wares of a certain and definite character. The writer who does not understand this purpose on the part of the editor, will be very apt indeed to receive a rejection slip in place of the much coveted check if he undertakes to place his name in its list of contributors.

One of the big differences between the publishing world today and that of when this article was written is the ease of self-publishing a work. Writers are no longer forced to aim their work at a specific editors. However, much of the advice remains the same. Instead of trying to write for an editor, authors are writing for fans of this or that genre. And research is easy - just check out the sales charts at any online bookseller to see what people are enjoying these days. If you are writing to sell, anyway.

A Word About Setting

By Sara H. Sterling

Originally published in the January 1916 issue of *The Writer's Monthly*

Every writer knows that there are three things necessary to every good short-story as to every good novel: Plot, Characters, and Setting. It matters not how interesting your characters, how full of atmosphere your setting, if your short-story lacks a plot, it is a short-story only in name, or in your opinion of it. You may have a most spirited plot, but if your characters are mere puppets, with the strings that move them very obvious, still you have not a real short-story. Lastly, you may have both a stirring plot and characters that seem actual flesh and blood, but if your setting, no matter how lightly sketched, is false or unconvincing, your public, if you ever reach it, will feel that something is lacking in your short-story, even though they may not be able to define wherein that lack consists.

Of these, setting seems to be the most difficult for a young writer to make effective. Nine times out of ten, the reason is that he has not a clearly defined idea as to what setting means. Asked by way of an exercise to outline a setting, he may write something like this:

"The shop was dark and low-ceiled. Clocks, ticking busily, stood on the shelves that lined the walls, and watches of many kinds rested in the glass cases upon the counter. An old man with a long gray beard sat near the door."

Now, this is setting, after a fashion; but when you have finished the paragraph, have you in your mind's eye a clear picture, or merely a somewhat confused mass of details? Here is the real test of an effective setting: Does the reader get a distinct mental image of the place you describe? Remember, you must yourself have that picture vividly in your mind's eye before you can make it live for him.

Let us take the paragraph just given, and see whether he can make it somewhat better.

"As Richard entered the clock shop out of the bright sunshine, twilight seemed suddenly to descend upon him. Shadowy, ghostly figures haunted the gloom, ranged in menacing rows upon the shelves around him. They seemed to mock or warn, in their monotonous ticking voices. Fainter voices, too, echoes as it were of the stronger ones, came from the glass cases on the counter. And who but the guardian spirit of the place—old Father Time himself, he seemed— sat near the door as ready to challenge."

Comparing these two versions, you will see first of all that no new detail has been added, though a character has been introduced, and the setting described from his point of view—always an effective method, although by no means absolutely necessary. We have used figures of speech to give vividness; and we have tried to create atmosphere rather than give merely a list of details. In other words, we have sketched a picture, not made a catalogue.

This illustration is, of course, a very brief and simple example of the point in question. Study Cynthia Stockley's stories, and note the unmistakable African atmosphere. Go to Kipling, naturally, for India; to Jacobs for the English sea coast town. Come nearer home, and read Mary E. Wilkins for New England, Thomas Nelson Page for Virginia, or any one of the numerous writers who have drawn so successfully for us the many and varied aspects of our great country. Read them critically; not only *feel* their effects, but see how they do it. And, here as elsewhere, note always that suggestion, although more difficult, is always a finer method than detail.

You may or may not agree with the example provided, but the point stands - setting is not just about accurately describing the physical nature of a time and place, it is also about instilling a feeling in the reader. And if you give a reader a feeling, he or she will imagine up plenty of their own details.

Where to Get Your Ideas for Plots

By Glenn H. Harris

Originally published in the March 1916 issue of *The Writer's Monthly*

A great many photoplay writers pay considerably more attention to the writing of the scenario than the method of obtaining the idea for the outline of the plot. The scenario is emphatically a technical proceeding which follows clearly outlined rules in the making. But since the scenario is dependent upon the idea for its very existence, it may be interesting to examine the best methods for the discovery and practical use of ideas.

Believe me, if you intend to make a little or a great deal of money by photoplay writing, you will not find it conclusive to success to sit down and wait for inspiration. Your inspiration should already be in front of you. In the first place, the more common sources of original ideas are the newspaper, the law courts, the office, and private lives. In these you find the germs for the best stories ever written, namely, those which are real human stories. Take the newspaper, for instance. In practically any edition one finds material and suggestions for a dozen first rate plots.

Glancing at a paragraph in a paper the other day, I was attracted to the heading "The Forgotten Bite." It was only the story of a snake charmer who was severely bitten, but so enthusiastic was he over his work that he forgot all about the bite and paid the penalty with his death. But what a splendid title and what possibilities there are in the theme.

Having scanned your newspaper carefully in the morning, mark with a blue pencil the paragraphs that suggest good plots. At the end of the day you can cut these out and paste them neatly in a scrap book kept for the purpose. If you are of a precise mind, you may index your suggestions in a variety of headings, embracing drama, comedy, farce, etc. But it may happen when you are on a car that ideas for plots present themselves. The best method is to make a rough note on a pad for the time, but when you reach home it is advisable to enter the idea in a small notebook which you may call your "Suggestion Book." This means that when you have a couple of hours to devote to your favorite hobby of plot writing you have before you well-stocked books containing the pith of the ideas culled from your own experience and observance instead of having to spend fifty per cent, of the time in racking your brains for the elusive idea.

A thousand different ways exist for authors to jot down ideas these days. Notebooks, of course, still exist, and there are a wealth of apps. Making a habit of collecting ideas when they occur will make sure you keep the best ones when you have them.

What is Interest?

By Barry Scobee
Originally published in the June 1916 issue of *The Writer's Monthly*

A hundred ingredients are used in making a piece of fiction, but fused into a single mass they mean one thing—interest. To be bought and published it must be interesting. The question, then, is how to supply that one necessity.

Our interest in life is founded on our longings and our needs; therefore a writer must play upon our hopes and desires as a musician plays upon an instrument—high and low, commandingly and beseechingly, softly and sweetly and triumphantly.

We are interested in a man we admire. Admiring him, we in a degree desire to be like him. We care, however—even the worst of us—only for the manly traits, conduct and aspirations. We cannot admire the weak, the coarse, the dishonorable; therefore, to make a story-hero interesting we must endow him with admirable, yet human, characteristics—ones with which we can sympathize or can imitate proudly.

This does not mean goody-goody, nice-little-man actions, nor does it mean a story-hero endowed with a heritage of misfortune for which we pity him—such as giving to his sister the last cracker in the cold, cold house though he himself is suffering from hunger brought on by sending his wages to the mother who is mistreated by her second husband. We should prefer to see the character hustle up two crackers and trounce the second husband. We do not care to be like the man we pity.

Let the story-hero meet misfortune or any other obstacle in a way we should like to do—with a grin, or a fighting fist, or a bit of cleverness that shows he is not an incapable. We can't be interested in the fellow we would not care to imitate in some respect.

A story-hero need not have all the virtues. In these the great picaresque heroes of fiction were woefully lacking. Villon, in Stevenson's "A Lodging for the Night," did not possess the sweet virtues of a tender and obedient bank clerk, but he did have something we admire, some cleverness and daring and an ability to care for himself. Just give the story-hero one big, wholesome characteristic we ourselves would like to possess, or fancy we do possess, and he is likely to be interesting. He may have more than one, but if a man is just average good and bad, and possesses one big, human virtue or ability we like him. Trying to arouse interest in a story-hero by contrast, by making him wholly good and his opponents wholly bad, is the work of an amateur. Just make the man human, with a character or characteristics we would try to imitate were we in his situation, and the story will twang a responsive chord in our hearts.

More than silly sentiment, more than catalogued vices and virtues, are needed to interest us. We must have our hopes and desires played and preyed upon. This is done, first, by giving the hero a touch of human kinship, by correlating us with the hero through something we admire or hope for in ourselves, then fingering up and down, back and forth, on the character's scale of failure or fortune.

Broadly speaking, it appears that interest is divided into two classes—human interest and heart interest. The former refers to courageous deeds, to setbacks manfully met, to hard fights well won; while heart interest refers to pathos and love. Both sorts are valuable, but seemingly human interest is far more popular. However, one of the best stories that ever appeared in the Saturday Evening Post was filled with pathos from beginning to end. But in addition, there was a heroic quality which won admiration.

Synopses of motion pictures in many trade magazines show that the pleasing stories have either heart or human interest appeal or both. Photoplays will not sell without it, though if the writer can put in the "unusual twist" of plot, and the strikingly new, so much the better. The same is true of stories for the fictions magazines.

The point, then, is that the writer should consider all plot germs from the view of giving the hero a part we admire—that we, in a similar situation, would wish to imitate. Finally, make heart interest and human interest the pivotal-points in writing fiction. Look at every plot first from that angle alone. It gives the struggling writer a solid base from which to work, from which to view the world, from which to write stories that sell. It will even be a valuable agent in moulding one's own philosophy of life.

There are still plenty of readers and markets out there for inspirational and aspirational protagonists.

Also, when Scobee here talks of "heart" and "human" interest, another way to consider those categories would be to say the main story question should be either one of achievement (will the protagonist do/get the thing?) or one of decision (will she say "yes" to the job on Mars?)

ARE YOU WORKING OR WISHING?

By Herbert C McKay

Originally published in the March 1925 issue of *Writer's Digest*

No, I am not a world renowned author. I am, like most of you, a beginner, fighting rejections and looking for the checks enclosed. For two or three years I worked haphazardly, keeping no copies, no records, in fact, writing a bit in a rush and mailing the result before I lost courage. About six or seven times a year I received a check for three or four dollars. I wonder how many others are doing this very thing now, perhaps not to such an extent, but to a certain degree?

About the only value I received from this aimless work was that I began to consider myself a writer. This idea resulted in the purchase of a copy of the Writer's Digest from a newsstand. I read it eagerly and it opened my eyes. I bought it regularly and then subscribed. I not only found valuable instruction, but many little hints and tips which have proved to be of the utmost value to me. Now I read every word of it.

A day came when I took myself to task. I had received the scientific education necessary to engage in bacteriology as a profession and was at that time following photography as a profession. Both of these subjects require earnest study and persistent effort before even passable proficiency is obtained. I determined to devote the same effort toward my writing. I carefully studied the magazines to which I wished to contribute. I did not merely look to see the type of material used, but I studied the length of the articles, the way the subject matter was arranged, and in short, tried to place myself in the editor's chair. That this policy was the only reasonable one, is attested by the fact that more than half of my articles at the present time sell on the first trip out, and also by the fact that my checks now range from fifteen to five hundred dollars. The latter amount is the largest I have ever received for a single manuscript—yet. Now, there was no magic in this. I merely stopped playing and buckled down to real work. I tried to give the editors what they wanted, and they did their part.

Many of you, and I include some veteran writers, are inclined to knock the editor. I wish to say that I have yet to find an editor who has acted unjustly toward me, and many of those who have accepted my work have gone out of their way to be courteous. When I read a letter or even an article in which the fledgling rails bitterly against the editor, I wonder if that writer has taken the trouble to think that in this country we have a population of more than a hundred million people, most of whom are served by one or more periodicals. Do these youngsters try to step out of their own circumscribed lives and secure adequate perspective? Do they try to imagine the rancher in the West, the debutante in New York, the village boy in Indiana, the orange grower in Florida, and a host of other widely differing types reading the product of their typewriters? The editor must have this perspective, and when he rejects a manuscript which is undoubtedly not suited to any stratum of our complex society except one so tiny that it cannot be seen by the naked eye. that editor has coals of fire called down upon his head by an angry contributor. Try to place yourself in the editorial chair and then ask yourself, honestly, if you would accept the manuscript in question. If you have the mental attitude of the reformer and wish to force your opinions upon the world in spite of all opposition—get out of the writing field! You may write of such prosaic things as cement machinery, but you must understand human nature and be broad enough to appreciate the other fellow's standpoint before you can succeed. Just remember this. The fanatic is rarely a person of real intelligence, and you must have a fair portion of that trait before you can appeal to the public by means of the written word.

To return to the question of the editor. I once wrote to Mr. A. H. Beardsley, the publisher of Photo-Era (who is also the author of a series now running in this journal) asking him if he would he interested in a series of articles dealing with a certain phase of photography. He replied that he would and I submitted the series. He then advised me concerning the matter of publishing these articles in book form and himself took up the matter with a publisher.

As a result, the publisher purchased the book rights of this series, and since that time has purchased a second book-length manuscript from me. This success was stimulating and directly led me into a broader field. I consider that this has come to me through the friendly efforts of Mr. Beardsley; efforts which ordinary business courtesy could never have demanded of him. Does this sound as if the editor is an enemy of the new writer? The truth is that the editor is the enemy of the writer who does not fully understand his subject.

Again. I sent in a short article to Popular Mechanics describing a toy I had constructed for children's use. This article occupied my time for possibly four hours. I received a check for fifteen dollars, but what was of more value was a personal letter from the editor stating that a check was enclosed, thanking me for the article and requesting further material. I sent another article to him and received twenty-five dollars for that.

These are but two instances. Publications which have used but two or three of my articles remit a check with a perfunctory note or form letter, both invariably worded most courteously. It will be found, however. that when your contributions to a given periodical have reached a fair amount, that the editor will be very glad to give you every advantage. You are important to his business. You supply the commodity which he retails, and he will not willingly cut off a promising source of supply.

Imagine that you are an editor! You have purchased a number of good articles from John Dolan, of Keokuk. On the morning in question you start reading manuscripts written in every conceivable manner upon all kinds of paper. Most of them are half-baked as to idea and unmentionable as to execution. At last you take up a manuscript written upon immaculate paper, to the first page of which is clipped by an easily removable clip, three well made photographs. You slip them off and you see neatly typed at the top of the first page,

"John Dolan, Keokuk, Iowa."

Do you plunge into it, reading eagerly? You do not! You breathe a deep sigh of relief, light a cigar, lean back in your chair and prepare to take your time reading it carefully. Why? You know that you will accept it, but you do this from sheer pleasure. It is a very real relief to read a well written, neatly typed article after wading through such a morass as you have passed and which lies before you. Ask any editor if I am not right.

Now how do I know this? I have never been an editor. I have never even seen the editorial office of any publication larger than a small county newspaper! I know it because I have tried to step out of my own personality and into that of the editor. I know how I should react to a given set of circumstances—and editors are human. Incidentally, if I am far wrong the editor of the Writer's Digest will reject this manuscript and you'll never be the wiser, so I can afford to be cock-sure.

In school you thought the teacher was your natural enemy. Don't take this attitude toward the editor. If you work and earnestly try to give him the material which his policy demands for his publication, he will meet you more than half way.

Another frequent alibi of the writer is that the editor rejects the matter which does appeal to him personally, setting himself up as a dictator of public taste. Have you ever stopped to think that the public pays good money for the magazines which are published in this country? Do you know any man who habitually purchases anything which is distasteful to him, if not forced to do so? The editor must give the public what it wants or get out! He has the responsibility of a business upon his shoulders.

Now boys—and girls, when next you get a rejection slip, don't damn the editor— don't even "darn" him. Get down and dig. Find out just why it was rejected. Correct that error and send it back. The slip you receive will bear the words:

"Pay to the order of..."

Again, these days many authors are not even submitting to editors, they are self-publishing and selling direct to readers. But the process is the same - only rather than research a magazine, you research a category and ask, "What are people buying in this category these days?"

SHOULD YOU WRITE POT BOILERS?

By Thomas H. Uzzell

Originally published in March 1925 issue of *Writer's Digest*

Former Fiction Editor of *Collier's Weekly*, Author of
"Narrative Technique."

One of the greatest shocks that come to beginning writers is the discovery that to earn money at fiction they must write "trash." Or at least the problem presents itself in that light. They go to the newsstand, select a few of the less literary, more obviously popular magazines, the ones they feel they should be able to sell to easiest, take them home, and read them with the object of learning "what the editor wants." Instead of being inspired, they are disgusted. They give these "magazines that entertain" to the cook or chauffeur or consign them to the garbage can and groan that they didn't know such stuff was printed; they would rather pick pockets than try to write it.

No greater encouragement is found by contemplating the very few high-brow magazines that print real literature. The depth of philosophy, the cultivated finish in style are too far beyond their modest powers. The market for such literary stories, moreover, is severely limited, since a half dozen good writers, if kept busy, could probably supply all the magazine short fiction consumed by the really discriminating reading public in America. In despair the literary novice asks: With the hundreds of short stories being bought and printed every month, why should I not be able to find a market for the kind of story that interests me, that is within my powers and that will pay me enough, say, to finance a trip to Europe or to buy me a nice, shiny, little Ford?

Why should the stories printed for the masses be so unbelievably bad? Should I force myself to write such bad stories? If I do, will my style be cramped forever and will I—lose my soul?

Such are the urgent questions faced more or less by practically every not-yet-arrived fictionist. Literary critics constantly stumble over the same issues and make needless mystery of their effort to solve them. The Los Angeles Times recently in inveighing against the authors of commercialized short stories, says: "They have made money for a while, but the greater things they might have done for literature and for themselves have been lost sight of. Contract-labor writing may be a good business but rarely art." The New York Evening Post issues this heart-breaking plaint:

> "There is a cascading torrent of commercialized sentimentalism. The so-called writer of American fiction is nine times in ten not a creator at all, but a shrewd individual possessed of a vocabulary, who has learned to feed the illusions of the multitudes. He looks not into his own heart, but into theirs, and with a skillful technique tells better than we can the crude stories of success in love or riches, of heroic self-sacrifice and escape which we all cherish and spin to ourselves between sleeping and waking. He exploits our rather weak imaginings, instead of creating new meat for us to feed upon. He is a parasite; his work is second-hand and second-rate, with a machine-made accuracy and no deep emotion whatsoever. Like the makers of the ancient ballads, these modern writers for the community give up their individuality when they compose. They sell their names for cash and henceforth are indistinguishable by anything else."

The problem of reconciling "commercialized fiction" with the ideals of literary art frequently agitates the instructors of literature and writing in the colleges and one of them has recently raised the issue to the dignity of a book. The author of this work, who is an instructor of short story writing in one of the eastern universities, asks in his subtitle whether short story writing is "an art or a trade." He seems willing to let the young writer devote himself to "stories that sell," provided that he admits that they are a deliberately inferior product that can never be termed "literature," but at the same time he insists that any writer really ambitious to attain large success should be a pure self-expressionist, making his standard always his own opinions and emotions and with no thought whatever to the "curse" of "catering to the public." This is a high, if not laborious, ideal and for some may be the way to success; but it gives little comfort to the writer who cannot, in either time or money, afford such expensive ideals, nor does it tell what will become of him and his writing if he eschews them at least for a time espouses the short-story-for-money-only.

Let us consider the pot boiler and what it means to write it. The argument most commonly offered against writing it is that it is not "worth-while." It is cheap, vulgar to the one who tries to write it, to the editor who buys it, and to the critic who deplores its effect on the "noble heritage of American letters." Comparison is always involved in any attempt at valuation and in this instance the standard of excellence is nearly always the masterpieces of writers of the past like Poe, Stevenson, and Maupassant. These authors are given as standard in the book mentioned above.

When we say "worth while" we mean worth while to someone. In this case—to whom? Obviously to the people like the critics and professors and others who derive pleasure from reading stories like those of Poe, Stevenson and Maupassant. How many such people are there and how many people are there who do not like such stories but who do like pot boilers? If, for rough statistical purposes, we group together the subscription lists of the purely literary magazines on the one hand and on the other the lists of all the all-fiction magazines and of the magazines with circulations over a million, ninety per cent of whose fiction can certainly be classified as pot boilers, we would undoubtedly find that there are something like thirty times as many readers of pot boilers as there are of literary stories!

From these calculations it would seem that if the question of what is worth while in fiction were put to a vote, the highbrow critics would be out-voted, thirty to one! The high-brow critic would undoubtedly object to this view of the matter and insist that the thing the low-brow reader wants is not good for him and that if his supply of cheap fiction were cut off from him and he were restricted to the classical commodity, he would be compelled to read the latter, his taste would be improved and he would be a greater blessing to his wife and children. This objection, however, looks like literary Prussianism. Such an edict would be no lovelier in the literary than in the political world. For my part, I can't see why the reader of pot boilers hasn't just as much right to determine his reading diet as anyone.

I feel sure that the confusion felt here by writer, critic and teacher results from the failure to realize that the problem of the commercialized American short story is a moral as well as a literary problem. It is a moral problem because it involve a question of life values, of what is "worth while," and such questions cannot be fairly solved by any *ex cathedra* formulation of literary standards or any appeal to anything as vague as "Is it art?" The way to solve a moral problem is manifestly to survey impartially all the facts involved and pronounce according to the logical demands of those facts.

Space is wanting here to review all these facts, but I can hint at some that are commonly lost sight of. The chief characteristic of the pot boiler is its appeal to the low intelligence. Why? The census of 1920 reports five million honest adult illiterates in the United States. Careful research discloses an equal number of dishonest illiterates, illiterates, that is, who did not report their inability to read and write; also ten million near-illiterates—a grand total of twenty million adult ignorami. We have in our midst, in other words, more full-grown people with the minds of children than the populations of Norway, Sweden, Denmark, Switzerland, and Scotland combined! There must be at least another ten million adults who can read but who could in no sense be considered educated. Most of these thirty millions either read or are read to and almost the only thing they are interested in is fiction. And their taste is for pot boilers.

The writer, critic and teacher naturally deplore this evidence of low intelligence and wish it were otherwise. The statesman and the reformer do likewise. But to declare that the best way to elevate this low intelligence of the people is to deny them all fiction except that which they cannot understand were a strange remedy indeed! The chief objection to this remedy is that it won't work. The only remedy worth considering is suggested in H. G. Wells' famous dictum to the effect that the world is now engaged in "a race between education and catastrophe." Education of the masses and not the suppression of pot boilers and editors who buy and print them, points the way out for the earnest social moralist who seeks one.

The chief purpose of fiction of all kinds is to entertain. In any search for the "worth-while-ness" of the pot boiler we must consider its value as entertainment to the consumer. To engage in the business —we can call it that—of helping to entertain thirty million of our fellow citizens is then not wholly to waste time and effort. Arrantly unjust is the New York Evening Post editor who calls the producer of such entertainment a "parasite." If, too, the editor feels that in reading them, his "weak imaginings" are being "exploited" and, to use his rather strange figure, he is not getting "new meat to feed upon," the thing for him to do is to read something else! As for the California editor who says that the writer could do "greater things" for himself if he didn't write for money only—well, possibly, but does the editor know how long we have waited to go to Europe or how convenient the little Henry would be just now? Also, how about newspaper editors and "greater things?" Not one editorial writer in five hundred in the United States writes with any other object than to please his boss, and as for the Los Angeles Times in particular—the history of past political campaigns in California is very well remembered!

So much for the moral problem. There is another thing to be said in answer to the campaigners against the writing of "commercial short stories." Most of them say, to quote the book referred to above, that "to the true artist the public is no problem," that Poe, Stevenson, and Maupassant were not concerned with financial returns and that "few magazines today would be tempted to accept stories like those of these past masters of the art. Amazing assertions! Where is the really great master in any art who didn't with painful attentiveness consider his audience? Michelangelo took his orders from the Pope; Velasquez flattered the court of Spain; Chaucer, deploring his small pay, wrote his poem,"Compleynt to My Empty Purse;" Shakespeare wrote for the "groundlings" in the pit; Paderewsky demands his prodigious fees. As for Poe, Stevenson, and Maupassant: the latter two, as anyone who has examined the bulk of their writings knows, seriously sacrificed the literary quality of very much of their later writings by unblushing devotion to what the public wanted and to the size of their pay envelopes. The thing that happened in their cases is what will happen in the case of nearly every fictionist: literary fame or cash? At the beginning of your career, you must make your choice.

Ideals of performance certainly should be held up before the ambitious young writers of America, but to establish as the sole ideal the writings of one, two, or three generations ago, even the best of them, is to restrict originality and risk literary stagnation. Magazine editors wouldn't today accept for publication stories like those of Poe, Maupassant or Stevenson, certainly, -and why should they? They can secure original stories much better than the average of these writers and occasionally they are lucky enough to find one as good as their best. Dogmatically I state this, for space is wanting to prove it, but proof could easily be had by anyone who actually reads the best stories being produced today and whose standards of excellence are not academically attached to the masterpieces which they glowed over in their impressionable youth.

Should the hedonist of today write pot boilers? The answer is bound to vary in each individual case, depending upon each writer's natural gifts, financial status, education and objectives. Especially does the answer depend upon his objectives. If you are certain that you have innate gifts adequate for the highest success at fiction and if you have provided or can provide a living without depending upon returns from your writing for several years, your best course very likely would be to eschew popular fiction altogether, to devote yourself to pure self-expression, to report the world as you see it. If, on the other hand, the possibility of your being able to pursue fiction at all depends upon your receiving a modest return from your writing, or if your only interest in writing is to earn as much money as you can by it, then common-sense would suggest that you begin at once to master the craft of the sentimental or "action" thriller! As for the rightness or wrongness of so doing—well, I think you will have as much "right" on your side as has the business man whose "bargain sale" carries prices higher than standard, the preacher who deals only in the "straight gospel" and avoids discussing the labor troubles of his wealthy parishioners, or the college professor who thinks he should be turning out Kiplings and Maupassants and instead teaches the formulas for "fiction that sells."

Problems involving the pot boiler issue are bound to occur which are more puzzling than the above simple cases. A young woman, one of my students, for instance, only last week asked me if she would be justified in continuing at the pot boiler writing she hated if by so doing she could put herself through college. When I learned that this was the only way she could get to college, I unhesitatingly advised her to do so. Another student of mine, a newspaper man, had before he came to me, succeeded with pot boilers until he had a record of fifteen straight with one periodical. In learning to break into the big league magazines, he had to cure the pot boiler habit, which to him took the form of melodramatic phrasing, and it took him a solid year of the hardest kind of grubbing before he finally landed with Collier's. On the other hand, I have in mind a brilliant college graduate who was utterly unable to write anything worth while until he had for a time forced himself, in spite of his disgust, to write a pot boiler a day with a murder to a page! He was plagued with the curse of "fine writing" and this "rough stuff" made any attempt at literary affectation ridiculous. So he was cured!

These remarks of mine must not be construed to be a defense of the pot boiler as a species of fine art. No one admires stories that appeal to the highest intelligence more than I do or is more anxious that I to increase their number in this humming land in which we live. My concern here is merely, if I can, to help the struggling writer see his way more clearly along the inevitably stony pathway which he must tread. Nothing in this world is more variable, quixotic, baffling, than the workings of the artistically creative mind and temperament. Constantly critics, teachers, and writers themselves succumb to the temptation to set forth mixed formulas for literary success, such as "Write only what pleases you," "Write what the public wants," "Never write for money," and "Avoid learning technique for it will kill your inspiration;" there is some truth in all of these adjurations, but any attempt to cling devoutly to any one of them will certainly produce more harm than good. The true guide for each writer who would succeed in the thing he attempts is to seek sound advice, keep an open mind, work hard and think clearly at each stage of the way.

I had to laugh as I read this one for the first time when Mr. Uzzell basically says, "There are loads of dumb people! Feel free to write for them, at least at first!"

Here's the same idea, but from a different mindset: It is perfectly fine to write to entertain regular people, totally ignoring the pretentious literary snobs of the world.

Later, he does restate what I believe to be a deceptively simple truth, which is, "The chief purpose of fiction of all kinds is to entertain."

All other writing rules should be second to that. Even if you want to spread a message, very few will ever read it unless the story entertains.

How to Make a Story Interesting

by John Gallishaw

From *Twenty Problems of the Fiction Writer*

"There is no answer to Boredom" —from Katharine Fullerton Gerould's article on the American Short-Story in the Yale Review for July, 1924.

At the outset let us recognize one fact. It is that creative writing is no longer the work of tyros. It is a profession, followed diligently by men and women as a means of livelihood. Because it is a relatively high-paid profession, it attracts yearly more and more competent followers. Steadily the competition becomes keener, and steadily the number of failures grows. The distressing feature of the whole business is that so often the line between acceptance and rejection is very slight. More frequently than their writers realize, stories are "almost good enough." needing only slight changes to make them acceptable. Slight though these changes seem, they are nevertheless essential. It was Michael Angelo who said "Trifles make perfection; and perfection is no trifle." Paraphrasing that, the aspiring short-story writer might well say to himself: "trifles cause rejection; and rejection is no trifle." It is the recognition of these "trifles" which characterizes the competent literary craftsman. Between the established writer and the beginner the only real difference is competence in workmanship: their material is the same, they differ chiefly in the quality of their craftsmanship.

In two respects you may judge the craftsmanship of a short story writer. The first is his mastery of structure; and is the measure of an author's capacity for Plotting. It implies an ability to observe, recognize, classify, and arrange his material. The second is his ability to present that material artistically. This second quality of craftsmanship includes the ability to blend the material of a story so that that reader is unconscious of the mechanism and is aware only of the effect. It is "the art which conceals art," and comes from knowledge of the resources of language: it is English Composition applied to the special requirements of the Modern Short-Story. These two abilities in a writer (Plotting and Presentation) should be developed side by side. Both can be developed, like all capacity, by practice. To say that one of these capacities is more important that the other would be as absurd as to say that for transportation purposes the vehicle is more important than is motive power; transportation cannot exist without both; so likewise a story cannot exist without both Plotting and Presentation. But Plot exists *prior* to Presentation. That is the only reason that I ask you to consider Plotting before taking up Presentation.

The first and most important thing for the writer of short-stories to keep in mind is that the short-story is a modern form as far removed from Poe's "tale" as the great S.S. Leviathan is from Fulton's first steamboat. It is not concerned with creating a single emotional effect; neither is it any story which is merely short. If shortness were the sole criterion, a chapter from a novel would be a short-story. The short-story writer's task is allied less closely to that of the novelist than to that of the dramatist. From the dramatist the short-story writer may learn one useful lesson.

The dramatist selects all the happenings for eventual Presentation in Meetings between two people. During these meetings there is an interchange of conversation. During such interchange, one of these people is an Actor and the other is a Stimulus to his actions. If a writer will once grasp this technical distinction, he will achieve a unity in his stories which will go far to keep the reader's interest at a high pitch.

Through the responses of the actor to the stimulus the character of the actor is shown. This is so in all sorts of fiction writing. The purpose of all creative writers, whether novelists, dramatists, or short-story writers, is the same: to show character through the reactions of the actors to the various stimuli of life.

It may be said, then, that the writer *presents* his actors in a series of meetings and interchanges. These meetings or interchanges may be classified as *Presentation Units*. This knowledge will permit you to amend your definition of a Modern Short-Story to read thus: A story is one person's account of things that have happened to him or to someone else, *presented in a series of meetings or interchanges.*

The mere rendering of a number of Presentation Units will not constitute a plot, A plot is made up of Crises or Turning points. The interest which is aroused in the reader from the Plot of a story may be, and frequently is, quite distinct from the interest which is aroused in a reader from the Presentation Units. Yet they are often combined and interwoven to such an extent that the reader cannot distinguish between the interest of the Plot and the interest of the Presentation Units. In general it is safe to say that from the writer's point of view, the material he deals with can be classified technically as Presentation Units which will be combined by him with Plot Crises in such a way as to make the two alternate.

Thus the story pattern finally emerges as a series of blocks. But within these blocks there is a further subdivision, which is fundamental.

1. Stimulus. (Most often another person.)
2. Actor.
3. Actor's response, characterizing the actor.

When we come to a discussion of the Scene as the unit, we shall see that in the ideally developed Presentation Unit, the interchange is the result of an actor with an immediate purpose encountering and clashing with another actor or force opposed to that immediate purpose. Thus in every scene the actor has a definite and immediate purpose, quite distinct from the actor's purpose in the main story. For that reason a scene or other Presentation unit may stand upon its own feet in respect to arousing the reader's interest.

On the other hand the interest which the reader feels in the Presentation unit will be enhanced as soon as he is aware that it has a bearing upon the plot of the Main Story, and realizes that because of what has happened in this scene or Presentation Unit there is a Crisis or Turning-point in the Story. The writer who is determined to arouse and hold the reader's interest will therefore select for his story such Presentation Units as will lead into Plot Crises in the Main Story.

Plotting therefore deals equally with the Presentation Units and the Story Crises. It consists of selecting happenings and arranging them into an outline or pattern for a story. *Presentation* consists of filling in the details of this outline so plausibly as to give the reader the illusion of reality, and so interestingly as to capture the reader's interest and to hold it throughout the story.

A short-story must have a Beginning, an Ending and a Body. The function of the Beginning is to set forth the story narrative problem confronting the chief actor, and such explanatory matter of setting, characterization, and prior happenings as may be necessary to lend plausibility and interest to that story narrative problem.

The Ending is concerned with showing the conclusive act by which the chief actor (or some force or forces set in motion by the chief actor) solves the narrative problem set forth in the Beginning.

The Body of the story is the *story-proper.* It shows the chief actor in a series of Meetings or interchanges, attempting to solve the main narrative problem.

The structural limitations of a story are, therefore, very simple. To adhere to these simple structural limitations is not a difficult requirement. The beginner and the established writer alike recognize them.

What you, as students of the short-story form, would like to know is why the work of one writer is accepted and the work of the other is rejected, when the two writers deal with material essentially the same. Sometimes this sameness in material goes so far as to embrace essentially the very same narrative problem in the Beginning, almost identical struggles in the Body, and very similar solutions of the same problems in the Ending. The reason for rejection lies in some lack in either the Story, which we classify as Plotting, or in the Scenes, which we classify as Presentation.

Since the accepted story and the rejected story could have been condensed to outlines which would have been remarkable for their resemblances, the reason for rejection could not therefore be because of faults in the Plotting. The reason for rejection must lie, then, in the Presentation.

The same happenings may be selected by two writers; but their *arrangement,* particularly in that portion of the story which we classify structurally as the Beginning, will cause one writer's story to be so *interesting* that it will be accepted, while the second writer's story will be rejected because it is dull.

More often than this, however, the reason for rejection is that the second writer *selected* the same happenings; but in *developing* them, in a series of Stimuli and Responses, his Presentation was ineffective, because it left the outline or skeleton too obvious to the reader, who had no sense of illusion. This is the greatest fault in Presentation. In most stories which are rejected the writers are too anxious to make the Story clear to the reader before establishing the *illusion of reality* through well-selected Presentation Units. On the other hand, when a story is rejected for lacks in the Plot, the writer has permitted himself to render Presentation Units, with no alternation of Story or Plot Crises. A writer who will keep in mind this necessity for alternation of Presentation Units and Story Crises *can make any set of happenings interesting*. Interest is the first requirement. It is a requirement dependent more often upon presentation than upon plot.

The comment most frequently made by publishers readers upon manuscripts which are "almost good enough" is "too slight— not enough story-interest." A story which is poor in all other respects will often be accepted because, despite its manifold faults, it possesses dramatic interest. Yet dramatic interest is not a matter of plot so much as of Presentation. A person taking up two stories whose plots in selection and arrangement of happenings are about the same, will be held by one because it has this quality of dramatic interest—which is compounded of plot interest and presentation interest—and bored by the other. There are different kinds of interest which every good writer should be aware of; yet day after day readers in editorial offices receive thousands of manuscripts which never ought to have been sent, and never would have been sent had the writers been cognizant of the devices and methods which are fundamental in creating interest. Fortunately, these devices are easily recognized: they are the writer's use of the Laws of Interest.

Interest, according to the dictionary, is *sustained attention*. To compel this sustained attention on the part of the reader is the task which confronts every writer who sets pen to paper. It is the reader who, seeing on the cover of a magazine the name of a certain writer, buys the magazine. It is the reader who writes to the editor, saying that he enjoyed a certain story; or, on the contrary, that he found a certain story dull. As Mrs. Gerould says, "There is no answer to boredom." The reader is, after all, the final judge. But it is axiomatic that you cannot sustain a reader's attention without first capturing it. To capture his interest and then to hold it is your never-ending task as a writer of the short-story. You see, you have two problems in regard to interest: to capture and to hold. To capture the reader's interest you must excite his curiosity; and curiosity is a single impulse to know more about something. This involves his attention; but as soon as he knows what he wishes to regarding whatever has excited his curiosity his attention flags.

Before this point is reached, you must excite another kind of attention, a kind which does not so easily flag: sustained attention. When the appeal to his attention is based solely upon curiosity, his unexpressed interrogation is "What is it all about?" On the other hand, with sustained attention there is present the added element of expectancy, which causes him to ask himself, "What will happen next?" and essentially and fundamentally, "Now what will this actor do when he encounters that stimulus?" With sustained attention there is present curiosity plus expectancy, which is what we commonly call Suspense.

Let us consider for a moment how you may use these two kinds of interest in the structural divisions of your story. These structural divisions are the Beginning, the Body, and the Ending.

The devices designed primarily to capture interest are those which you will have to use in the Beginning of your story. By the Beginning is meant not the first few paragraphs merely, but sometimes as large a proportion as one-half or two-thirds of the whole story. The Beginning consists of two subdivisions: One of these is the Situation, or narrative problem, through which the reader is made aware that the chief actor is confronted by a problem demanding for its solution, action on his part.

The other subdivision of the Beginning is the part which causes writers the most difficulty, because of failure to understand, completely, its function. It consists of the explanatory matter necessary to capture the reader's interest *by making the Story Situation or Problem both interesting and plausible to the reader.*

The function of this Explanatory Portion of the Beginning is to set forth the Condition or State of Affairs which precipitates the problem. In some stories the Main or Story Problem is so interesting, in itself that without explanatory matter, it can be presented at once, and be depended upon to capture the reader's interest. It is then said to be an *Intrinsically* interesting Story Situation.

In most stories, however, the Main or Story Problem becomes

interesting only after its importance has been built up for the reader by the Explanatory Matter: the Condition or State of Affairs which confronts the chief actor. It is then said to be a *Synthetically* interesting Story Situation.

Even in the case of the *Intrinsically* interesting Story Problem, Explanatory Matter (the Condition), although delayed in its introduction, must be included. It is essential to make everything clear to the reader. That is for Plausibility. It is also necessary to set forth this Condition facing the chief actor in order that the reader may feel that his interest had been roused justifiably. For clarification, you may wish to set before your reader certain biographical details which will help him to understand the actors; you may wish to impress upon him some special quality in the background or atmosphere; or you may feel—and this is by far the leading reason —that for a full comprehension of the importance, or difficulty, or urgency of the Problem confronting the chief actor, the reader should be made aware of certain prior happenings, and especially of the likelihood of failure and of the probability of opposition.

In Plotting the Beginning, therefore, you will keep in mind its two sub-divisions.

1. The Main Narrative Problem or Story Situation, which is interesting either intrinsically or synthetically.
2. The Explanatory Matter, making the reader aware of the Condition Precipitating the Story Problem.

It is safe to assume that if a reader is sufficiently interested to read through to the Body of your story, he will continue to read. Your chief problem, then, is to capture his interest at once. This you will do by appealing to his *curiosity,* pending the moment that you can count on his *sustained interest* in the Meetings or Interchanges that make up the Body of the story-proper.

Particularly is this true in the case of the Synthetically Interesting story, when the Condition must be set forth before the Story Situation can be presented. In this kind of story— and the great majority of stories fall into this category—everything depends upon the interest of the Presentation Units. Only after the reader has read the Presentation Units does he become aware of the importance of the Main Story Situation or

Problem.

This demand for interest you must keep in mind throughout your story, from the opening sentence to the closing word; but particularly in the explanatory Matter of the Beginning. It is this Explanatory Matter which is most often depended upon to catch the reader's interest. It is the Beginning of the story which, capturing the reader's attention, most often determines for him—and this includes the professional "reader" in the editor's office—whether or not he will continue to read the story.

Now the ultimate Beginning of any story, that part which comes at once to the reader's attention, is the title. From the point of view of interest, a good title is, then, your first consideration in arousing the reader's interest. The title should be arresting, suggestive, challenging. Kipling's "Without Benefit of Clergy" has all of these requirements. So has Barrie's "What Every Woman Knows." So has Henry James's "The Turn of the Screw." So has O. Henry's "The Badge of Policeman O'Roon." So has John Marquand's "A Thousand in the Bank." Octavus Roy Cohen is particularly apt in this respect. The moving picture producers know the value of an interest-compelling title; in fact, they carry the question of title to excess—into the realms of questionable taste. But their titles do *arouse interest.* And for the moment you are concerned only with *interest.* You may say definitely that the first device for capturing interest is in the *selection of a title* which will cause the reader to pause, which will whet his *curiosity.*

This desire to excite the reader's curiosity will guide you always in selecting and arranging the materials that go into the Beginning of your story, that portion setting forth the story Problem and its involvements. No matter what sort of story you propose to write, regardless of your stage of progress in fiction-writing, your materials will always be the same: Stimuli, Actors, and Character Response forming a narrative pattern.

Yet you may use all of these materials in the Beginning of your story without exciting the reader's interest. The arrangement may be wrong. The reader "doesn't know what you're driving at." So you see, the materials cannot be arranged indiscriminately.

In order that the reader may find the Beginning of a story interesting, these materials must be arranged in such a way that the reader is aware that a character is facing a grave crisis in his career, is confronted by a problem demanding action on his part, or is in a dilemma from which he must extricate himself, or is in a position which makes it necessary for him to choose between courses of conduct.

There is always a narrative problem when there is *something to be accomplished, or some decision to be made.* Unless one of these elements of Purpose or Indecision is present there is no narrative problem. This is a fundamental requirement in the Beginning of any and every story. That is what makes it a story.

However, in the completely developed Scene, this same element occurs. A narrative problem is a fundamental requirement of a scene as it is of a complete story. A scene has all the elements, in miniature, of a complete story. Usually they are, in scenes, problems of *purpose.* So that we may say then that there are *scene purposes* and a Story Purpose. Either may be used TO CAPTURE A READER'S INTEREST.

While the title is the first device by which you attempt to arouse the reader's interest, you will ensure a let-down of this

interest unless you make him aware, within the first few hundred words, approximately, of a Purpose. Ordinarily, this Purpose will be a Scene-Purpose. Its appearance will cause the reader to ask himself a question: "Can A succeed in getting information from B.?" etc.

Just as a hostess gives the guest soup, or an hors d'oeuvre to stimulate his appetite for the main dish, you furnish this scene to prepare the reader for the Main Story. You may have to provide him with more than one scene before you feel that he is ready for the Main Story Situation. But your fundamental task, in capturing your reader's interest is to make him aware, at the earliest possible moment, consistent with plausibility, of a Main or Story Situation, quite apart from the scene purposes, which will thereafter condition the actor's responses. This you will succeed in doing when you make the reader aware that *the chief actor is called upon to Accomplish something or to make a Decision.*

But at this point you will find yourselves puzzled by the fact that among the material which you have available, while there are plenty of happenings which show that there is *something to he accomplished or decided,* you do not find that something of sufficiently compelling interest to lead you to appraise it as a possible Main or Story Situation. And here a great and fundamental truth in regard to the Laws of Interest begins to dawn. Let me illustrate: If you are sitting by the shore of a quiet lagoon while a dog is swimming lazily from shore to shore you may be trying to cause the dog to fetch a stick. Although in your attempt to direct the dog there is something to be accomplished, you are only mildly interested. But if, instead of a quiet lagoon, there are windswept breakers hurling themselves against a precipitous cliff, and the dog instead of swimming lazily, is so exhausted that his attempts to reach the place you indicate seem difficult of accomplishment, your interest grows. Your interest will be increased if the dog is your dog and a valuable animal that has won many money prizes at dog shows. Further, if you have agreed to forfeit a large sum of money should the dog not be on hand at a certain hour, now very near, for another show, you will be still more interested. And if, instead of sitting quietly, you are pinned under an overturned automobile, your interest is intense. But it will be still more intense if you are trying to cause the dog to swim to the assistance of a small five year old boy, equally exhausted, and that boy is your son whom you love devotedly.

In the first instance you found yourselves mildly interested, in the second intensely interested. In analyzing the reasons for the differing intensity of your interest you will discover that in the second instance *more depended upon what happened.* And that is the great fundamental secret of interest— *Importance. A Situation involving purpose or choice is interesting in proportion to what depends upon it.* The more important the accomplishment the greater is the promise of Disaster in case of failure. The more that depends upon the decision or choice to be made, the greater is the promise of Disaster if the wrong decision is made. And any Situation, to a person of imagination, has potential fiction importance, because much may be made to depend upon it. When you fully comprehend and can supply this Law of Interest you hold the key to plotting.

Your third method of capturing interest, therefore, lies in making sure that the situation is Important, either Intrinsically in itself, or Synthetically, because of what depends upon it. In Will Payne's story "Paradise Island" the situation (the thing to be accomplished) is Important in itself; a man sets out to kill another man: all the explanatory matter or the involvement making up the rest of the Beginning gains a borrowed importance from it. In Frank R. Adams's story "Spare Parts" on the other hand, the situation (the thing to be accomplished) is unimportant; a man sets out to drive an automobile from Los Angeles to St. Louis. In exact contrast to Paradise Island, the explanatory matter, or the involvements, making up the rest of the Beginning, lend an importance to the Story situation. One is an Intrinsically important Story situation. The other is a Synthetically important Story situation.

In the Intrinsically important Story situation, the main situation being interesting in itself gives plot interest at once to the story, and can be presented before the explanatory matter. In the synthetically interesting Story situation no such gain of plot interest would result if the main situation were presented before the explanatory matter, because the plot interest is not apparent until after the reader becomes aware, through reading the explanatory matter, of the involvements which give importance to the main situation.

In your search for Story situations which are interesting you will be helped by what journalists call "a nose for news." As your purpose is to arouse curiosity, you will do well to inquire as to what things people are curious about. Everyone remembers how, in the first years of the great war, Americans read avidly all that they could about the World War. Then there was a slump; curiosity was sated. It had ceased to be "news" temporarily. Now that a new and more "human" aspect of the conflict is being dealt with, the war is again "news." Almost everybody is familiar with the story of the veteran newspaperman who explained to the cub reporter: "If a dog bites a man, it isn't news; but *it is news* if the man bites the dog." Only recently a man whose business in life is editing the news summed up news values very cleverly. He said:

> 1 ordinary man + 1 ordinary life = 0
> 1 ordinary man + 1 ordinary wife = 0
> 1 ordinary man + 1 auto + 1 gun + 1 quart = News
> 1 bank cashier + 1 wife + 7 children = 0
> 1 bank cashier - $100,000 + 1 chorus girl = Head-lines.

The explanation, of course, is that the things which have no news value are the things which are usual; those which have news value are those things which are unusual. So you come to another method of stimulating or creating interest— *the Unusual.* This quality of being unusual may be in the Story situation (the thing to be accomplished or decided) or it may be in the status of the character who is confronted by the situation. In "The Face in the Window" by William Dudley Pelley, although the situation is unusual (a woman sets out to capture a dangerous, escaped murderer), in the status of the woman there is nothing unusual. She is an ordinary New England villager. But ordinarily, New England village women do not spend their time in such a pursuit. On the other hand, in "Western Stuff" by Mary Brecht Pulver, the story situation (the thing to be accomplished) is usual enough (a woman finding that another woman is monopolizing her husband's attention, sets out to regain him). The status of the character, however, is unusual. She is the queen of the rodeo riders, a type of person one does not meet very often. In selecting as material unusual situations for main or story narrative problems your test will be the very simple test of asking yourself if, out of a hundred people you know, how many have to meet that problem. In selecting unusual types, you will make a similar test. Out of a hundred people you meet on the street, how many are that special type.

It is in this interest in the unusual that you find the explanation of the great vogue of the "local color" story in America. People are interested in certain places, places in which they have been, or places in which they would like to be. Certain regions and certain places are symbolic. Most Americans are interested in New York City. A few years ago the majority of stories had their setting in New York. It was the mecca of many people who had been there or were hoping to go there. People read about places with which they would like to be familiar. Men sweltering in cities like to read stories of the Maine woods, of the Rockies, of the "great open spaces where men are men and women are mates." Out of twenty stories read, which I selected at random recently from current magazines, *fifteen* had settings in foreign countries; only two were laid in New York; one in a small college town in New England; *one* in Hollywood; and one was laid on a Western ranch. New York is no longer in the lead. Thus it goes. One after another, certain regions are discovered, are exploited, have their vogue, and fade out, to give place to some more interesting region. After a while they cease to be interesting because they cease to be unusual; they have become usual, the glamour is off them; familiarity has bred contempt. What applies to places in this respect applies also to the people in the stories. A writer finds certain kinds of people interesting; on paper he makes them live. Kipling wrote about the Anglo-Indian; O. Henry wrote about New York shop-girls;

Ben Ames Williams writes about New England countrymen; Octavus Roy Cohen writes about the negroes of Alabama; H. C. Witwer writes about prize-fighters. The public is tremendously interested; other writers less original and less competent, noting the success of the first, try unsuccessfully to portray the same kind of people; soon there is such a succession of them that the reading public tires of them; they cease to be people and become types; the pages of the poorer fiction magazines are full of them; the moving pictures particularly swarm with them. Beginning as individuals, they prove on examination to possess little individuality; they have ceased to be unusual.

Many writers producing stories about unusual people against unusual backgrounds are amazed to have those stories rejected. If they understood the Laws of Interest, the reason would be clear. Setting and people have of themselves no narrative or plot interest. Setting and people are stimuli. A plot is responses arranged as crises. But the amateur writer will continue to write standardized background stories. They run to types. In the United States this standardization has reached a point where there is a public for particular kinds of plots—the Western story, the Sea story, the War story, the College story.

The significant thing about this division into types of backgrounds is not so much that there is a public for each type as that there is a large public who never read certain type stories, because those stories, depending for their interest upon their background, are more or less stereotyped as to plot and have ceased to be interesting. In many cases readers await eagerly the appearance of a certain type of story, continue to read that type for a year or so, weary of it; and turn from it in search of some other type. To those readers, the first type has ceased to be *unusual.*

It would appear from all this that it is an axiom that the device to capture interest is the *unusual.* Yet you will remember that I told you that five out of the twenty stories which I examined achieved their interest while dealing with the usual American background. Actually there was something *unusual* either in the actors or in the happenings.

Still, you find competent artists like Edna Ferber, who write extremely interesting stories apparently about usual people in usual surroundings doing the most usual things. In such cases you will discover that the artist has thrown new light on an old subject. Interest is achieved by unusual interpretation of a usual phenomenon, or the unusual adaptation of a usual incident. And so you come to your fifth device for capturing interest—the apparently usual is conceived as unusual. It is not a question of phrasing, it is a question of originality of conception.

In a story by Edna Ferber which appeared in the *Red Book* a few years ago there is an example of this. A New York shop-girl comes out of her dingy home looking marvelously attractive. That was the material Edna Ferber had to work with; but her imagination conceived the comparison of the dainty girl and her dingy surroundings with a butterfly emerging from a chrysalis.

In Irvin Cobb's story, "We of the Old South," which appeared in the Cosmopolitan for November, 1924, the material he had to work with was a girl who had borrowed her name one place, her accent another, etc. Cobb's imagination took this out of the commonplace and made it unusual by likening her, in the vernacular of men who deal in motors, to an "assembled product."

Comparison and Imagery are qualities of the Imagination. It is the Imagination which enables the writer to recognize the *unusual,* particularly when it is not obviously apparent. By this ability, which will help you to add a great deal of interest to the part of every story which is normally the dullest part,— the explanatory matter of the main situation,—your rank as a creative artist will be judged. To be a writer you must be at once a psychologist and an advertising expert. You must understand the value of different appeals. Kipling created an India that no one knew existed. But he got his interest not so much by the unusual that was India, as by the unusual that was the Englishman in India or the Irishman in India— by a juxtaposition of the known against the unknown— *by contrast.* You all know that on a black velvet gown a string of pearls will show up better than against a background of their own color. A *contrast* or a juxtaposition of opposites, then, is your sixth method of achieving interest. This contrast may be between the main actor and the setting.

In *Collier's* for February 6, 1926, May Edgington in "Purple and Fine Linen" made use of this kind of contrast when she showed a woman begging in a district of London sacred to old and dignified clubs. This contrast may also be between the main actor and another actor with a prominent rule. Irvin Cobb in "We of the Old South," made use of this kind of contrast by throwing together a typical, simple, ingenuous, kindly, old Southern Colonel and an equally typical chorus girl. Almost automatically in this juxtaposition of an actor and an unfamiliar background, or of an unusual type person against the usual type person, or of the unusual type and the usual problem, or the usual type and the unusual problem you come to your seventh method of capturing interest —the foreshadowing of conflict, of difficulty to be overcome, of disaster to the cause.

It is important at this point that you do not confuse the two different kinds of interest, presentation interest and plot interest. The interest aroused by the title; the interest aroused by the juxtaposition of opposites; the interest aroused by imagery; the interest aroused by the unusual conditions and unusual characters, and even the interest which comes from the promise of difficulty, conflicts or disaster are all subsidiary to and dependent upon story or plot interest. Plot interest is concerned with making the reader aware of the importance of narrative turning points or crises. The other types of interest are utilized to keep the reader from being bored, while he is being given the information which contributes to the unusualness or importance of those narrative turning points or crises, of which the essential one is the main crisis or the main Story situation. For I cannot too often reiterate that without an important situation (something important, either intrinsically or synthetically, to be accomplished or decided) there can be no story. Equally, without a story there can be no story or plot interest. All other interest is presentation interest.

The comment of the editorial reader upon the "almost accepted" story, you will remember, was "not enough story-interest." Real "story-interest" does not come until the Body of the story when the reader is aware of the Story Situation, and the conflict begins. Not until conflict is shown in the form of an encounter can there be sustained "story-interest." But in the Beginning, while you excite the curiosity of the reader in regard to the outcome of the main situation (the main thing to be accomplished or decided), you also entice him to continue interested by holding out to him the *promise of conflict, difficulty, or disaster*. This is plot interest, and distinct from his interest in the scenes themselves. You have, therefore, you see, counting the title, seven ways of capturing the interest of your reader in the Beginning of your story and one of these (the seventh—the foreshadowing of difficulty, conflict, or disaster) contains in addition to curiosity, the quality of expectancy, which makes your story dramatic.

1. A title which is arresting, suggestive (in the better sense) and challenging.
2. A Story situation (something to be accomplished or decided).
3. Importance of the situation or its involvements, made clear in Scene or Scenes.
4. The inclusion of something unusual in the Story situation or in the chief character.
5. Original conception or interpretation so that the apparently usual is made unusual.
6. A contrast or juxtaposition of opposites.
7. The foreshadowing of difficulty, conflict, or disaster, to carry interest over to the body of the story.

Up to this point I have concentrated upon indicating to you the possibilities of arousing or capturing interest. From now on I shall ask you to abandon the consideration of that kind of interest which is *curiosity,* for the consideration of that kind of interest which is *sustained attention.* I shall ask you to turn from that portion of the story which is technically classified as the Beginning, to that portion of the story which is technically classified as the Body. The Beginning, you must remember, does not mean always merely the first few paragraphs: it includes that portion of the story which sets forth the Main situation confronting the chief character and such explanatory matter of setting, characterization, or prior happening as are necessary to give plausibility and interest to that situation. This main situation may precede the explanatory matter or it may follow the explanatory. A good Story situation, judged in regard to interest, is one growing out of a great crisis in the life of the main character, with much depending upon the outcome, and which demands instant action from the character. It is interesting in proportion as it is important or unusual. Its primary function is to show that something is to be accomplished or decided by the main character, involving the probability of difficulty or disaster, and primarily of conflict with some opposing force or forces.

Once the reader's interest has been aroused by the prospect of conflict you will be unwise to delay the appearance of the opposing forces. At the earliest moment consistent with plausibility you will arrange a meeting between your main actor and one of these forces. And keeping in mind the necessity for plot interest, you will arrange that the outcome of this meeting will form a new crisis by confronting the hero with a new situation; with the necessity for trying again to bring about a solution of the narrative-problem, so that the reader is made aware that until this new situation is disposed of, the outcome of the main situation is still in doubt. This new crisis or turning point in the Body of your story will hold for the reader an importance borrowed from the original Story Problem presented in the Beginning of your story.

Whenever the editorial reader says "not enough story-interest" he means one of two things: that the story lacks a sufficient number of such crises to keep the reader in suspense as to the outcome of the story, or that the meetings which intervene between the crisis are not sufficiently interesting in themselves to hold the reader's sustained attention until a new crisis is reached. In the first case, the lack is in your plotting; in the selection and arrangement of your happenings, so that the reader is aware of crisis. In the second case the lack is in your presentation, which usually means that you have not enough clash in the meetings which you select. This is what the average man or woman means when he says "I didn't like that story because 'nothing happens.'" Most stories which are rejected have this basic fault. They do not have enough encounters; and the reader is, therefore, unaware of any sense of clash of opposing forces. Or they do not keep the reader in suspense by making him feel that success is unlikely. With the encounters under way you have story interest. In the well constructed story these encounters will be the outgrowth of the main or story situation.

In presenting the meetings or interchanges which make up the Beginning you achieve story interest by making the reader aware of the main or story situation and showing the prospect of conflict. In presenting the meetings or interchanges which make up the Body of your story, you will be concerned with showing the reader that conflict in a series of encounters. Throughout the presentation units which make up the Body of your story, the reader sees that the actor is engaged in an encounter or in a series of encounters as a result of his attempt to solve a Story Problem of which the outcome is in doubt. The inclusion of this conflict or clash of opposing forces is, then, the eighth method of creating interest. It is the chief method of holding interest. Yet, no matter how vividly you can present these meetings and interchanges of opposing forces, you may still receive rejection slips if your plot sense is so poor that you fail to indicate to the reader that the result of every such meeting or encounter is a crisis in the central attempt of the main character to solve the problems raised by the main situation, such crises or turning points forming new situations which still leave the ultimate outcome in doubt.

Then each conflict is made interesting by expectancy, by a desire on the part of the reader to know what is to happen next. Thus story-interest can be aroused by either crises or meetings, but preferably by both, because story interest comes from suspense, which may be in relation to the outcome of the actor's immediate purpose in a single meeting or to the outcome of the Main situation of the story as a whole. Always, however, in the Body of your story the Kind of interest which you seek to excite is the interest of sustained attention or what is commonly known as "suspense."

As soon as you leave that portion of your story which is classified as the Body, and begin the consideration of that portion which is classified as the Ending, a third type of interest appears. In the Beginning of your story you arouse the reader's interest by hinting of encounters to come; the interest is chiefly the Interest of Curiosity. In the Body of your story you postpone gratifying the curiosity which the Beginning arouses, by keeping the reader in doubt as to the ultimate outcome of those encounters; the interest is the Interest of Suspense. But when the curiosity is gratified, and the suspense over, there remains the task of making the reader feel repaid for the time he has given to the reading of your story. He must be left with a feeling that his curiosity was justified by what eventuated, and that the end was worth waiting for. He must be left with a sense of satisfaction regarding the outcome, a feeling that given the actors and the circumstances the only ultimate result of the encounters is the result you have shown. The Ending need not necessarily be the conventional "happy" ending. It is required only that it seem inevitable. The interest in the Ending of your story is the Interest of Satisfaction.

In achieving this third type of interest, there are two devices used especially. Of one of these O. Henry was the great modern exponent. He is remarkable for the adroit twist which he gives to his plots; so much so, in fact, that he is today remembered chiefly because of that, whereas his real claim to distinction rests upon no such flimsy foundation. He had a great eye for contemporary types. But before he portrayed them they were not types. Nevertheless, he is now cited chiefly because of his extraordinary mastery of one of these devices—the use of the unexpected. The Reversal of the original situation confronting the main character has always been a favorite method of causing in the mind of the reader the sense of satisfaction as to the outcome. It is made dramatic by surprise. Henry Fielding, whom we commonly regard as one of the originators of the English novel, phrased this Law of Interest very neatly, thus:

"... within these few restrictions, I think, every writer may be permitted to deal as much in the wonderful as he pleases; nay, if he then keeps within the rules of credibility, the more he can *surprise* the reader, the more he will engage his attention, and the more he will charm him."

O. Henry's story, "The Cop and the Anthem" is a typical example of the use of the unexpected by the reversal of the situation. The tramp who sets out to be arrested, is arrested after he has changed his mind; after all the ordinary causes for arrest have failed to land him in jail, he is arrested for listening to church music.

The next device upon which I have not touched is one which, although extremely effective, is not employed nearly as much as it might be. You have seen that an incident of no intrinsic interest can be given a synthetic or built-up interest through combination with other incidents. But a synthetic interest may be given to an incident or happening by its meaning. An incident meaningless and undramatic in itself may become very meaningful and striking in proportion as it is significant or *symbolic*. Wilbur Daniel Steele, in a story called "When Hell Froze," causes a woman to plunge her hands into a pan of lye to symbolize her admission of infidelity to her husband. In "The Sign of the Lamp" Thomas Burke causes one of the characters to pull down a window shade, an act insignificant in itself, but rendered significant because it is a signal to the police that a certain fugitive is hiding in the room. In the Beginning of a *Saturday Evening Post* story a girl jokingly tells her step-father that she is proof against emotional disturbances and that if she ever does fall in love she will consider it a sufficiently important occasion to send her step-father a telegram. At the close of the story she says"I must send a cable to Cyril." When ordinarily a man says, in reply to an invitation to drink: Thank you, I don't drink, it is not especially interesting; but when it signifies a definite result of a struggle against dissipation it becomes significant. There is a striking example of this in the closing sentence of the story "Sunk" by George F. Worts. This tenth device for achieving interest is the inclusion of the *symbolic* or *significant act.*

The twelfth and last of the devices for sustaining interest is the one which is usually the result of practice. You know that frequently you read, and find interesting, a story whose plot is by no means strikingly original; you will read again and again a type of story in which the same characters appear; you will even look forward to stories in which the people and the happenings are deliberately distorted. You enjoy these stories because of the author's gift for language. There is something original or charming in the phrasing. It is, as Pope puts it, "What oft was thought but ne'er so well expressed." This originality or charm of phrasing may run throughout the story. It may be used while you are exciting Curiosity, or Suspense, or Satisfaction. This method of achieving interest is not to be confused with the third method, the unusual interpretation of usual phenomena, which comes before phrasing and is in no way dependent upon phrasing. Interpretation is a part of Plotting; phrasing is a part of Presentation.

In applying these Laws of Interest to your work, you will, of course be careful not to attempt too arbitrary a distinction as to the scope of the different Kinds of Interest. While it must be apparent that a certain kind of interest belongs primarily to the Beginning or the Ending or the Body of your story, it must be equally apparent that it cannot be confined to that portion alone. For example, although the use of the unexpected outcome is ordinarily employed in the Ending of a Story to show the ironic reversal of the Story Situation set forth in the Beginning of the Story, you may make use of this quality of unexpectedness in the ending of a Scene. In that case it will form a crisis in the Story Pattern or Plot, and may occur at any point in the progress of the Story—in the Beginning or in the Body. It may come *at the conclusion of any meeting* at any point in the Story. It may even occur during a meeting.

At the conclusion of this discussion I have prepared, for your information a diagram. It will help you to understand the main divisions into which a story falls. I have represented each of these main divisions as a block, and within each block is a statement setting forth the *functional* purposes of that particular division. On the left of each such division is a list of the devices normally employed by the writer to enlist and hold the reader's interest.

This diagram is intended to be used by you as a standard of

specification against which you may check a story you write. You will be helped vastly by reading stories in current magazines, in an endeavor to see by what devices the writers succeed in enlisting and holding interest.

You will be very much interested to discover that your stories may be made interesting by the employment of the devices indicated. You will also learn a great deal by attempting to determine, in reading other people's stories, the exact point at which you become seized with a desire to skip. You will discover, usually, that you will read a Scene between two people without loss of interest; but that your interest will drop, if, at the conclusion of the Scene there is no indication of a crisis in the Plot. You will see for yourself, in this way, that a Scene in a story becomes interesting in proportion to what depends upon it. Realizing this analytically, your task is to put it into effect, *creatively*. Stories will not come to you ready-made. A condition may exist which is *unusual;* but it will not of itself, constitute a Story Situation. Your task is to select or invent Important Main or Story Situations. You will first have to vizualize it as Something to be Accomplished by an Actor, or as Something to be Decided (Some choice to be made) by an Actor. If the Story Problem so raised is not in itself interesting, *make it interesting* by making much depend upon it, by causing it to become important to the actor, and preferably make it both important and unusual. Once you grasp this essential, the road is clear ahead; until you grasp it, everything is chaos. **It is not easy.**

Facility in invention comes only from practice. Many people never become good at plotting, in the sense that it is easy for them. Their chief reliance must be upon Presentation. But Presentation is not easy. It is so tiring that many people rebel against the labor it entails. That is not the time to abandon effort. Many people find their muscles complaining against physical exercise. Ordinarily, the more the muscles complain, the more you need that exercise. So it is with exercises of the imagination. The imagination, like everything else in nature, grows by what it feeds upon. Most of you will find the inventive side of Plotting difficult at first.

But that should not discourage you. Although, at first, problems of plotting appear appallingly difficult, they become increasingly easier. Keep your goal clearly in mind. The reader's interest must be captured and held. In attempting to do this, you are in competition with *thousands* of others. And the reader has ample choice. He won't read your story unless it interests him. If he is bored he'll stop reading. Remember "There is no answer to Boredom."

THE APPLICATION OF THE LAWS OF INTEREST TO THE DIFFERENT DIVISIONS OF THE MODERN SHORT-STORY

Type of Reader Interest Sought

DEVICES

1. A Title. — Arresting, suggestive, challenging.

2. A Situation. { Some feat to be Accomplished, or Some Course of Conduct to be chosen.

> Happenings presented to make clear to the reader that the Story Purpose (Accomplishment) or Story Problem, (Decision), calls upon the chief actor to engage at once in action.

CURIOSITY: A SINGLE DESIRE TO KNOW MORE ABOUT ANYTHING.

3. Importance of Story Situation. Intrinsically or Synthetically through foreshadowing.

4. Difficulty, Conflict, Disaster.

5. Unusualness of Story Situation; of Actor's status.

6. Impressions by Contrast.

7. Impressions through unusual conception of the apparently usual, through comparison or imagery.

> The Condition precipitating the Story Situation. Rendered in Presentation Units or in Author's Interpolations to make clear to the reader that the Accomplishment or Decision can come only when the chief actor has
> (a) Overcome Difficulty
> (b) Engaged in conflict with Opposed Forces.
> (c) Averted Disaster.

THE BEGINNING

8. Dramatic Interaction of OPPOSING FORCES that clash about immediate purposes in Scenes. This clash brings about Plot crisis at the end of each scene.

> A series of Presentation Units in which the character-traits of the different actors should emerge.
>
> The attempt to overcome a Difficulty.
>
> The attempt to overcome an Opposed Force, and
>
> The Attempt to Avert Disaster (all foreshadowed in the Beginning) are developed.
>
> Each such attempt causes a crisis or turning-point in the Story Plot.

SUSTAINED ATTENTION: SUSPENSE AS REGARDS THE OUTCOME OF STRUGGLES.

THE BODY

9. The Unexpected.

10. The Symbolic Act.

> Made up of Presentation Unit or Units showing the Conclusive Act of the Plot, by which the Main Actor (or some force acted upon by him) meets the Story Situation.

11. Significance.

> Plus the significance, ironic or otherwise of the Conclusive Act. (Sometimes shown as a Sequel.)

A SENSE OF SATISFACTION IN REGARD TO THE OUTCOME OF THE STORY.

THE ENDING

12. Permeating the Whole Story— originality or charm of phrasing or treatment.

This chart can be found online at vintagewritinginstruction.com/laws_of_interest

I absolutely love this. Find a way to hook the reader, keep them, then finish strong.

Drama in the Short Story

By John Gallishaw

From *Twenty Problems of the Fiction Writer*

The Scene as the Unit

More and more, as you make a careful study of the modern short-story, you will become convinced that the ability to create an interesting and convincing illusion of actual life is the ability which is the mark of the highly competent craftsman. Certain Laws of Interest, as definite as the Laws of chemistry or physics, applied to your material will help you in the selection and arrangement of that material so that in presenting it you will create the illusion you wish—the illusion of actual people in actual places, reacting to stimuli in such a way that the traits or characteristics are made clear to the reader.

From a study of the Case Book you will have learned that there are four definite narrative turning points or crises in every story. One of these, the Story Situation, occurs in the Beginning; two, the Furtherances, and the Hindrances, occur in the Body; and the fourth, the conclusive act, occurs in the Ending of the story.

A glance at the chart accompanying the Lecture upon the Laws of Interest will show you that a Main or Story narrative situation (that is some feat to be accomplished or some choice to be made), even though intrinsically unimportant and uninteresting, can be made important and interesting by adding to it the promise of conflict with a difficulty; the promise of conflict with a dangerous opponent, and the promise of a conflict which will be necessary to avert disaster or defeat. When a Story situation is thus made important it contains the quality of being Dramatic. The hint or foreshadowing of difficulty, of opposition, and particularly of disaster, makes any undertaking hazardous and, therefore, Dramatic. Obviously, then, if this hint of conflict is dramatic the conflict itself must be even more dramatic. Equally, if the Promise of Disaster or Defeat is Dramatic the appearance of that Disaster or Defeat itself is even more Dramatic.

It will be apparent that just as each of the narrative turning points falls naturally into one of the three great divisions of Beginning, Body and Ending, so do these qualities of Drama. The Promise of Conflict, with difficulties, with opponents, and with impending Disaster or Defeat lends drama to the Beginning; the conflict itself lends drama to the Body, and Disaster or Defeat lends drama to the Ending. It is obvious, of course, that in every conflict there must be two opposing forces, and that necessarily Disaster or Defeat for one implies the avoidance of Disaster, (success) for the other. Thus the Ending will be dramatic if it contains either Disaster or its avoidance.

You will now begin to see that in Plotting your stories you will have to include not only Narrative interest, but Dramatic interest. From what you will learn about Setting and Actor Images, you will see that you must include also Impressions of people, places, and things to achieve the illusion of reality. In addition to Impression there is the Emotion which is Feeling, and which comes from the readers awareness of an actor responding to a stimulus.

Summed up, then, you must cause the reader to feel emotion by showing the actor's responses in a narrative pattern of dramatic material which gives the impression of reality.

Impression will come from setting and actor images. Feeling will come from characterization. In observing and classifying material you will keep those categories in mind. Because you realize that with the short-story writer life is dynamic, you will accustom yourself to think of your material in terms of happenings.

If you see the sun rising over the Matterhorn, or if you hear a train whistling in the distance, or if the pungent odor of creosote smites your nostrils, if the breeze blows dust into your eyes on land, or salt spray into your mouth at sea, these happenings you classify as happenings which illustrate setting. If you see a stylishly dressed, tall, graceful girl of twenty, with even features and curly hair, hurrying along the street, you have observed a happening which you will classify as an image of an actor. If you see a man kicking a crippled dog or twisting a woman's wrist, or rescuing another from drowning at the risk of his own life, or giving his last cent or his last bite of food to help a comrade in distress, you will classify these as happenings *illustrating character.*

Yet, on the other hand, you have not observed anything which, standing alone, contributes to that vitally necessary quality in a story which we call the Plot or the Narrative Pattern. It is important that you see this distinction clearly. A story gets its emotional value (its impression and its feeling) from Setting and from Characterization, but in its plot it deals only with narrative turning points or crises; a series of these crises properly arranged making a narrative pattern and giving it narrative or plot interest.

An important category, then, under which you must learn to classify the result of your observation is: *happenings which illustrate narrative turning-points or crises.*

Sometimes a happening may be made to contribute to both the emotional effect and the narrative effect, A happening which you may select as a happening illustrating setting, may perhaps also be a happening which forms a turning-point or crisis in the narrative pattern or plot. For example, a man by striking an enemy with an ax in a moment of passion illustrates his *character;* but this action may also be a *turning point in the plot.* The breaking up of the ice upon a river may illustrate setting, yet it also may be a *turning point or crisis in the story* of a person whose safety depends upon the stability of that ice. Herein lies the difference in attitude toward material between you, as a writer of fiction, and the writer of nonfiction. The writer of non-fiction is concerned with rendering setting and character. He sometimes is dramatic. So are you, but, while rendering setting and character you will render them as much as possible in terms of narrative and dramatic crises.

You will train your observation, therefore, to extract, wherever possible, besides impression and emotion, the narrative and dramatic value from closely linked happenings. In your presentation of your story you will always keep this in mind, and you will, whenever any element is lacking, make the additions necessary to bring about this result. As there can be no story interest until there is a narrative pattern, you will be especially receptive and perceptive toward those happenings which can be classified as contributing to the plot: as being turning points or crises having narrative quality.

As soon as you begin to think of your happenings in terms of narrative crisis you have swung out of the first phase, which is the observation of material. And as soon as you have reached the point of classification, you have begun to plot. Plotting includes, in addition to the selection and classification of material, the arrangement of the selected material into a pattern. But this arrangement comes as a result of selection and rejection. What I wish to emphasize to you now is the indisputable fact that, if you know how to observe, you can gather in one month of well-directed observation such a quantity of happenings that you will be amazed that you could ever have offered as a reason for not writing the excuse that you had nothing to write about.

It is enlightening to see what a professional writer has to say in this regard. H. G. Dwight, in *Mehmish* (Stamboul Nights) says:

"The fillip of life, for me, is in the small permutations and combinations of incident that make up the lives of us all. And I have often picked up a trait of character or a turn of phrase from a Mehmish that has stood me in good stead with a Pasha. Did you ever realize, however, what an art it is to tell the story of one's day? Women sometimes have it to perfection. We call it gossip, but it is the raw material of literature, and it is better than the glum silences that fill so many habitual tete-a-tetes."

As I pointed out to you earlier in this course, the "fillip of life" for you will be the happenings which do not seem especially worth collecting and recording to the non-fiction-writer. You may collect them from your own observation, or you may secure them from others. So long as they give the reader the impression of reality the source doesn't matter.

This freedom of selection widens your scope of available material very greatly as you think in terms of plot or narrative interest. You will be amazed at this scope if you just run over in your mind those happenings which you can classify as crises or turning-points that you have experienced, or that you have observed, or that you have been told about, or that you have read about in the past two weeks. Here, for example, are some of the crises which apart from your own experience you may have seen, or been told about, or have read about.

1. A neighbor tells you that her son, who is poor, has fallen desperately in love with a wealthy girl who has many more eligible suitors, and has sworn to win her.

2. A young man tells you that he has put all his available capital into equipment for a trip to the newly discovered Canadian gold-field where he hopes to make his fortune.

3. You learn from a young man, whose brother has been brutally and mysteriously murdered, that he has sworn to discover and kill the murderer.

4. A woman who is hurrying for a doctor for a child who is critically ill, discovers that a railroad train will crash against an unexpected obstacle if she does not stop to warn it, thus losing precious minutes.

5. A newspaper man, whose creed is that all news must be printed regardless of who suffers, is given an item telling of his son's arrest for embezzlement.

6. A prohibition agent who needs money to make good his son's defalcation, is offered a bribe by makers of poisonous whiskey.

7. A child tells you that he has been promoted in school.

8. You hear that a pugilist has just knocked out an opponent.

9. You read that an arctic explorer, whose ship has been nipped between ice-floes, has abandoned his expedition.

10. A young man offered a bribe to betray an employer decides to remain loyal.

Now, if you will analyze these crises, you will see that they fit into different categories. The first three all show a determination to accomplish something. A young man wants to win a girl. A young man wants to make his fortune. A man wants to discover and punish an unknown murderer. The classification, then, is "some feat to be accomplished."

The next three all show a choice to be made between courses of conduct. The woman may save the train passengers or her child. The newspaper man may suppress or publish. The prohibition agent may accept or refuse the bribe. The classification, then, is "some course to be chosen."

As soon as you can make your readers aware of something to be accomplished or of something to be decided by an actor you have a narrative situation. (A Narrative Problem.)

Numbers 7, 8, 9 and 10 can all be classified as conclusive acts. They show that something has been brought to a conclusion. As a reading of the Case Book will show, in a story of either decision or of accomplishment, narrative turning points, or crises, then, consist of the moment when the reader becomes aware that there is some necessity for the character to accomplish some feat, or to decide between courses of conduct, and when he becomes aware that something has been brought to a conclusion of either decision or accomplishment, therefore, a conclusive act. These are narrative turning points. Until the reader is made aware that the actor must accomplish some feat or decide some purpose he is not aware of any narrative interest, or narrative problem.

The narrative problem causes the reader to ask himself a "narrative question." As soon as the reader becomes aware of some feat to be accomplished he phrases, either consciously or subconsciously, a question: "Can the chief actor succeed in accomplishing his purpose?" As soon as the reader is made aware that the character has to choose between two or more choices of conduct, he phrases for himself a narrative question:—"What course of conduct will actor A decide upon?"

In the first case the narrative question is one of accomplishment; in the second it is one of decision. It is the narrative question which determines the narrative situation. There can be no narrative situation without a narrative question, of either accomplishment or decision.

It is quite obvious that the character's attempt to accomplish any feat must either succeed or fail, and that eventually this must be made apparent to the reader. As soon as the reader becomes aware of this success or of this failure, his interest in that particular narrative question ceases. Equally, a person who is torn between the desirability of different courses of conduct must eventually come to some decision, even though that decision be to postpone action for the present. Sometimes this postponement is forced upon the actor by an outside force; by some other person or by some pressing immediate necessity. In effect, this decision to postpone, whether voluntary or involuntary, is *conclusive* as far as the necessity for decision is concerned; a course of conduct in regard to the immediate narrative situation has been decided upon definitely. The reader's interest in that narrative question raised by that particular narrative situation ceases.

As soon as the reader is made aware that an actor's reaction to a stimulus causes him to ask himself a narrative question, the reader's interest is aroused. As soon as he is made aware that the narrative question is answered his interest ceases. Obviously, an outline of a story could be made up of units containing situations arousing narrative questions and of answers to those narrative questions. Sketched it would be like this:

DRAMA IN THE SHORT-STORY

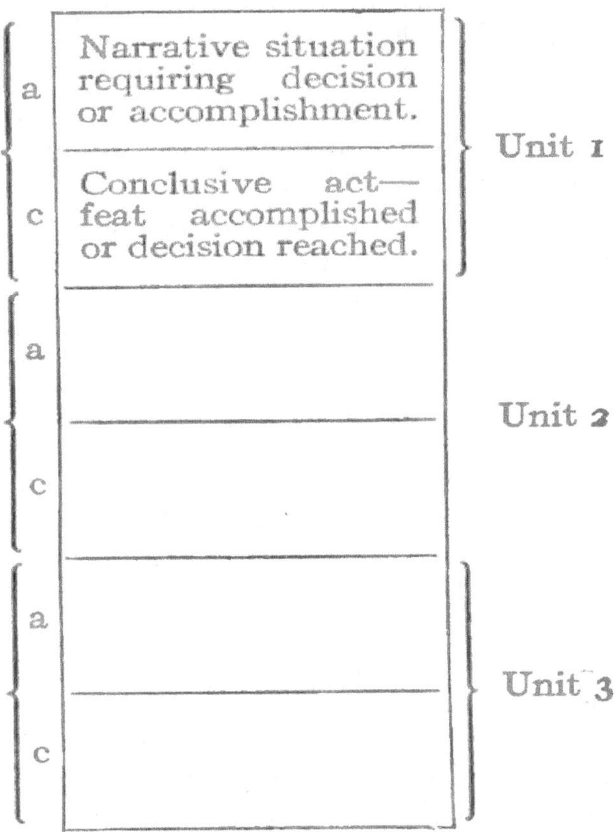

Of course, this is a good start for the structural sketch, but there would be practically no emotional interest. There would be no sense of characters in action, and virtually no suspense; for no sooner would the reader have his curiosity aroused as to the outcome of any situation than that curiosity would be satisfied through a realization that the narrative question raised had been answered. The reader's interest in any narrative situation will last only so long as he is unaware of the outcome of that situation. For that reason the conclusive act which makes him aware of that outcome must be delayed as long as possible if there is to be any suspense. There is only one way to delay this answer, and that is by causing the character to meet a force or forces which will either passively or actively delay or hinder the occurrence of that conclusive act of decision or accomplishment; in other words, by the introduction of other stimuli to which the character can respond. The more responses shown, the greater will be the possibility of your success in stirring the emotions of your reader.

You cannot go far in visualizing any story without seeing an actor or a number of actors in action, responding to stimuli.

Of necessity, everything an actor does or says or thinks must be that actor's response to a stimulus. This is inescapable because everything that any actor ever does, or says, or thinks is his response or reaction to a stimulus. Thus, you see the object of observing in terms of stimuli and of response. It is axiomatic that no actor in a story can respond to a stimulus without becoming aware of that stimulus, so that basically, every character response of an actor to a stimulus is a *meeting* with a stimulus. Therefore, the only way to delay the answer to a narrative question is to make the reader aware of a meeting of a character with a stimulus, or stimuli, *after* the reader has raised that narrative question in his own consciousness, and *before* the reader is made aware of the conclusive act which answers for him that narrative question.

Instantly, you will have become aware of a new category into which to place the results of your observation; the category of meetings. The category of "Meetings" thus embraces three kinds of meetings. It is essential that you learn to distinguish between these kinds of meetings, because each one has its own special purpose, and for that reason I am going to ask you to employ a definite nomenclature which will enable you to avoid any difficulty of misunderstanding. For the first kind of meeting, then, the one which serves to show merely the reaction of the character to a stimulus, the stimulus not reacting upon the actor, I shall ask you to employ the term "incident." The incident is the single act of a single actor reacting to a stimulus, which is itself inactive to the extent of having no design upon the character, thus: "at the stroke of five John Morton laid down his pen." The stimulus is the *condition* of five o'clock striking. The reaction of John Morton is to lay down his pen. In the meeting which we shall hereafter classify as an incident there is no interchange between the stimulus and the actor. The actor alone is responding. That is to say, he reacts; the stimulus does not react. As soon as there is an interchange, there is a meeting of another kind. For example, "Upon the stroke of five, John Morton, noticing that his friend and fellow-worker, Bob England, was still bent over his ledger, walked across the office and whispered under his breath"Come on, old boy, the tocsin has sounded." "Right you are," his friend responded cheerfully, "I'll just put these books in the safe and be with you in half a minute."

In this type of meeting, two forces meet amicably; there is an interchange without clash, each force forming the stimulus to which the other responds, and each one actively and designedly reacting upon the other. John Morton responds to the sight of Bob England; that response itself becomes the stimulus to which England's speech forms the response. For the purpose of mutual and definite understanding between instructor and instructed, we shall hereafter in talking about this type of meeting of two forces involving "interchange without clash"—employ the technical term "episode."

There is another type of meeting in which two forces meet, but in which the interchange involves clash or conflict. If John Morton crosses to his friend Bob England and suggests that the two go out, only to find that England is irritable and gruff, and is himself roused to retort, then there is a meeting with clash, both forces being stimulated by the action of the other. To describe such a meeting we shall employ the technical term "encounter," which is a meeting of two forces, both actively reacting, *with clash*.

There are, therefore, three kinds of meetings, the incident, the episode and the encounter.

1. The incident is the single act of a single force; it may present either a stimulus or a response. "As soon as he spied the policeman Henry tiptoed across the street" is an incident; it is the single act of a single force. The force is Henry, the act is his tiptoeing across the street. It shows his response to a stimulus, which is the sight of the policeman. That stimulus is presented as an incident. "He (Henry) spied the policeman."

2. The episode is the meeting of two forces without clash; thus:

"As soon as he spied the policeman, Henry tiptoed across the street, and coming up behind the officer, tapped him lightly on the shoulder.

"The other swung around sharply, his hand reaching instinctively for his hip pocket.

"At the sight of Henry he relaxed: 'Yuh frightened me fer a minute' he said.

"Henry leaned close 'I'm going up the street for about two minutes. Keep your eye on the door of that garage, and if anybody comes out, blow your whistle.'

"The policeman nodded understandingly. 'Don't be long' he said. 'There may be something doing any minute now'."

3.   The encounter is the meeting of two forces, with clash; thus:

"As the moon rose slowly above the low roof of the garage, Henry could see the policeman crouching in the angle between two buildings. The officer's back was turned, and his gaze was fixed upon the door of No. 29.

Tiptoeing with infinite caution, Henry crept up behind him. He was almost upon the bulky figure when the policeman, apparently satisfied by his scrutiny, turned around without haste.

At the sight of Henry he stiffened, his hand reaching instinctively for the revolver in his hip pocket. Even after he had recognized Henry he did not change his attitude.

" 'Don't get excited,' said Henry, I'm just going up the street a minute.'

"The policeman continued to gaze at Henry coldly. 'You are not/ he said.

" 'Why?' inquired Henry.

" 'Because I got me orders that nobody leaves this alley before the Chief gets here.'

" 'Good heavens' said Henry, in annoyance, 'that didn't include newspaper men.'

" 'It goes for everybody,' said the other shortly.

" 'What'll you do if I go ahead?'

" 'Try it and see,' said the policeman, and continued to regard Henry without smiling. When he saw that Henry had apparently no intention of retreating he produced the ugly looking automatic, and pointing it at Henry's stomach, said meaningly, 'Get back where yuh came from, and if yuh make a sound, I'll plug yuh.'

"It was clear to Henry that the officer meant what he said. There was no profit, he thought, in being shot; so he stepped back, gingerly, to the place he had left."

You are now in a position to add to your sketch of the presentation unit, some clarifying information, by placing after the word Meeting, the explanatory words incident, episode or encounter. The incident is the irreducible minimum. Perhaps the most enlightening instruction a teacher of short-story craftsmanship could ever give is to drill into those people who have difficulty in developing material the comprehension of the basic importance of the incident. Every time you render for your reader an account of a force in action you have begun to write a story. Plotting consists merely of putting that incident into its proper category. It is a simple thing to record an incident to be used in a Story, because it involves merely showing an actor responding to a stimulus, that stimulus being another actor.

You may build that incident up until it becomes an episode by causing the response of the first actor to form the stimulus to which a second actor responds; and the episode may be expanded to the extent to which you keep up the friendly interchange or interaction. Always, however, it will be by the addition of more incidents.

Just as it is possible to build up an incident into an episode, by the addition of other properly selected incidents, so is it possible to build up an episode into an encounter, by the addition of further incidents introduced to show that hostility has entered into the interchange. The incident is always the lowest common denominator.

Arranging incidents so that they form episodes presents no problem. Adding clash to such episodes to produce encounters is comparatively simple; it demands only the most elementary knowledge of craftsmanship; even the mediocre writers do it instinctively. By adding clash they manage to add dramatic effect, but they could keep on doing so forever and they would not achieve narrative or plot interest.

Narrative or plot interest is contributed to any meeting *within the story* in the same way that narrative interest is contributed *to the story as a whole*—by preceding the meeting by its own situation and following it by its own conclusive act. This structural unit of situation—meeting—conclusive act—we shall call a "Scene." A unit within the story, it has exactly the same functional divisions as the whole story.

1.   The raising of a scene narrative question to capture the reader's interest by making him aware of a scene situation.
2.   The delaying of the answer to that scene narrative question through the readers' interest in the interchange which follows.
3.   The answering of the scene narrative question raised, in such a way that there is no longer any doubt in the reader's mind as to the outcome of the interchange.

It is the second of these divisions within the scene which at the present moment concerns you most closely. It may be an incident, an episode, or it may be an encounter. It is so unlikely to be an incident that you can afford to ignore an incident as a possibility for your consideration and narrow down your investigation to the episode and the encounter. Each of the "scene" units that make up the story, you can say with assurance, has the same functions as the complete story, and it has, like the complete story, a Beginning, a Body and an Ending, corresponding to the functional divisions of situation, interchange, conclusive act; the interchange being the Body.

The unit of structure which I sketched for you, now becomes

enlarged by the interpolation of another subdivision, and sketched, looks like this:

DRAMA IN THE SHORT-STORY

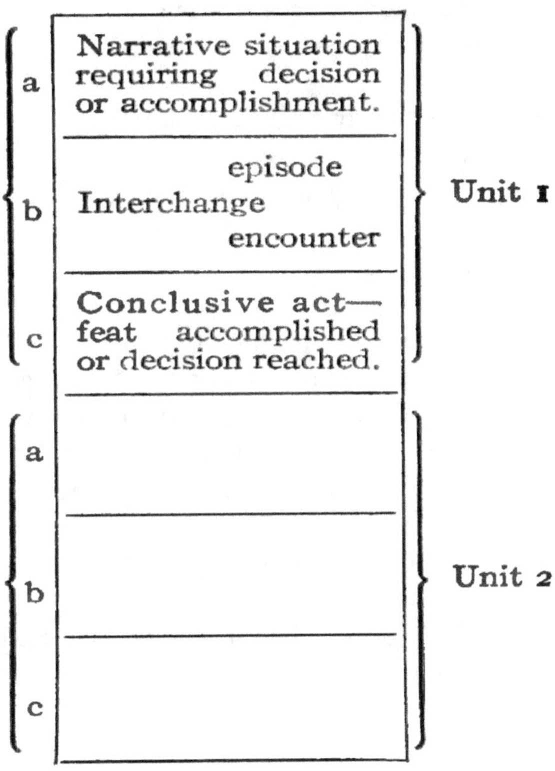

It is the interchange within this scene unit to which you must devote your best efforts. Upon your ability to present it interestingly and convincingly you must eventually stand or fall. You must, if you are to be successful, apply to it the Laws of Interest. An interchange, you know, may be either an episode or an encounter. But, if it is an episode it cannot be dramatic, because an episode *has no clash*. It cannot be narrative because if there is no clash there can be no alternation of Furtherance and Hindrance, and, therefore, no uncertainty. As soon as you add clash to the interchange you almost inevitably add alternation of Furtherance and Hindrance. As soon as you add Furtherance and Hindrance to the interchange you achieve clash. Thus drama adds narrative and narrative adds drama. But as soon as you add drama, which in the Body is conflict or clash, you change the episode to an encounter. Thus we see that the Body of the narrative unit within the story, which we shall hereafter refer to as a scene, may be either episodic (if it has no conflict or clash), or dramatic (if it has conflict or clash). We now can draw some very definite conclusions that will go far in clarifying your task.

First. There are two kinds of situations—Story situations and Scene situations.

Second. The Story situation (the main situation) projects the actor into a series of attempts or interchanges, each one having its own scene situation or purpose.

Third. A Scene situation is followed by a single attempt or interchange. Thus, a man's purpose to win a girl would form a story situation. In the course of his attempts to win the girl, the man might need two hundred dollars. His purpose to borrow the two hundred dollars would form the scene situation.

Fourth. The Body of a scene may be an episode. In that case the scene is an *episode scene.*

Fifth. The Body of a scene may be an encounter. In that case the scene is a *dramatic scene.*

Sixth. The incident (the single act of a single force) is the basic structural unit. It may be expanded gradually into

1. episode
2. encounter
3. episodic scene
4. dramatic scene
5. complete story

The dramatic scene contains all the elements of the complete story. It is a miniature short-story. The complete story is made up of the number of these scenes. Clearly, then, if every story consists of a number of scenes, in order to be able to write a short-story you must first be able to

(a) Distinguish between Story situations and Scene situations.
(b) Build up an incident through its different phases until it becomes a dramatic scene.
(c) Present the dramatic scenes convincingly, so that the characters

of the actors emerge against an impression of Time and Place.

Throughout each dramatic scene, through the actor's reaction to different stimuli, you will make his *character* clear to your reader. The technical devices for illustrating character you will become familiar with from your study of the Lecture on Characterization. In the long run, you must realize that *characterization is everything* in a story, and that your real reason for familiarizing yourself with structural devices is to acquire complete control of methods in order that you may not be hampered in rendering character through the medium of the Modern Short-Story.

The chief aim of this course is to teach you the fundamental architectural conception of a short-story as a series of blocks, each block being the equivalent of a scene. However, since no architectural conception of a story will of *itself* produce a story, there must be, within that architectural conception, the breath of life which comes from *characterization* of actors responding to stimuli.

The value to you of knowing just what is a scene is inestimable. It is a smaller unit than the complete story, yet in architectural conception it is the same. Being the same in essence as the complete story, the dramatic scene gives you opportunity for developing your plotting ability as well as your presentation ability. It includes:

An impression of Time and Place, and Social Atmosphere.

An impression of an actor's appearance.

An impression of the stimuli to which the actor responds.

Since the largest number of your scenes will be scenes in which the opposition to an actor is furnished by another actor, the second actor and his responses will be the stimuli to which the first one will respond. Therefore, the first step in a dramatic scene of that kind is to bring the two actors together— To achieve narrative interest you show your reader that one of the actors has a purpose (we shall leave for later consideration the scene requiring choice). To achieve dramatic interest you show your reader that the other actor is opposed to that purpose. So far you are dealing with the Beginning of the narrative scene. In plotting it you will keep in mind that the purpose of actor A may bring about the meeting with Actor B. For example, if A wants to borrow ten dollars from Actor B he may go to actor B's house or office to meet him. On the other hand, actor A may not think of attempting to persuade B to lend him ten dollars until after he has run into Actor B casually on the street. In this case the purpose grows out of the meeting; in the other case the meeting grew out of the purpose. That is entirely a matter of choice with you as author, depending upon your conception of how things would have happened in real life.

In plotting and presenting a dramatic scene, remember that your detail must give the impression of reproducing real life. In giving your actor a purpose, be sure to reproduce the ordinary purposes which actuate people on every hand. In that way you will achieve verisimilitude, or the appearance of truth. You will find as you observe closely that when one actor meets another his purpose is to secure information; to convince the other of something the other is doubtful about; to persuade the other to adopt a course of conduct; to impress the other with his own importance or lack of importance (if he is trying to evade a tax, for example). As soon as such a purpose appears, the reader is caused to ask himself a scene-narrative-question.

Can Actor A secure information from Actor B?

Can Actor A convince Actor B?

Can Actor A persuade Actor B to adopt a course of conduct?

Can Actor A impress Actor B?

When there is physical clash, the reader asks himself, "Can Actor A overcome Actor B or Force B?" Once you have enlisted the narrative interest of the reader in the purpose of an actor in a scene, and have added dramatic interest by the hint of conflict, which will come in the interchange between the chief actor and the opposing actor, you must take swift advantage of that interest to present the interchange in such a way that the outcome of the actor's attempt to achieve his purpose is in suspense. Every speech or act of Actor A will be intended to accomplish his object. If this attempt promises success, there is a Furtherance of the Scene-narrative-question.

If from a year's study of this course you mastered nothing but the fact that every attempt of an actor to bring about a narrative purpose is a Furtherance to the purpose and to the scene narrative question raised in the mind of the reader by the knowledge of that purpose, it would be a year well spent, provided you coupled with it the knowledge that the furtherances are introduced to give plausibility to the *Hindrances* which give the dramatic interest through their promise of ultimate disaster or defeat.

Therefore, to ensure a dramatic scene you must be sure to follow every Furtherance (that is, every attempt of an actor to bring about his immediate purpose in that scene) with a Hindrance. To do this you will show the opposing actor attempting, by his speech or act, to prevent the chief actor from accomplishing his purpose. If this attempt promises failure for the chief actor in that immediate purpose, there is a Hindrance to the Scene narrative question. This interchange between Character A and Character B will, in the well balanced scene, occupy the largest proportion of the space.

Finally, in completing the scene you will show the conclusive act of the scene which brings the interchange to a close. This conclusive act will show that the actor whose purpose raised the scene narrative question has either abandoned his purpose or achieved his purpose. It will be either Defeat or its avoidance. The answer to the Scene narrative question will be either Yes or No. It can never be "perhaps," because even though the encounter between Actor A and Actor B results in a draw, it is a defeat for Actor A. He has not achieved his purpose.

Keeping in mind the analogy between the scene and the story, you will add whatever significance there may be as a result of the encounter:

(a) As it affects the Character. For example: "Although victorious, he felt strangely dissatisfied."

(b) As it affects the Opposing Force. For example: "He glared at Thompson from the corner into which he had been thrown. It was apparent that, although defeated, he was not conquered."

I shall say nothing at the moment about the relation of this step in the scene to the main narrative problem of the story. I shall leave that until we deal, later, with the general problem of plotting the story as opposed to plotting the scene. It is sufficient for you to remember now that the first rate modern short-story is made up of a number of dramatic scenes. Clearly, then, this being the case, in order to be able to write a short story, you must first be able to plot and write good dramatic scenes.

As soon as a writer has mastered the problem of enlarging encounters into scenes he has achieved narrative interest. Perhaps it would simplify this if I were to say that the problem is one of enlarging meetings into scenes. Narrative interest is added to any meeting by preceding the interchange by a scene purpose showing that the response of an actor to a stimulus is the determination of the actor to accomplish something, and by following this interchange with a conclusive act. The actor whose purpose gives the scene its narrative interest may be any actor in the story. There are, therefore, the following steps to each scene:

1. To bring actor and opposing force together
2. To show that one has a purpose
3. To show interchange
4. To show conclusive act
5. The effect. (By this step you tie your scenes together into a story.)

The fifth step sometimes appears to be missing. This is frequently because there is so much of it that it forms by itself another complete scene. An actor in one scene may have failed to secure a loan of ten dollars. The fifth step may consist of his reflections that he was unwise to ask. It may consist of a visit to another person whom he tries to persuade to give him a job. This visit will itself form another scene.

Gallishaw's ideas in this chapter are clear forerunners to some of what is taught in Dwight V. Swain's "Techniques of the Selling Writer." In Swain's teachings, and in many related frameworks, The steps to each scene are restated as Goal, Conflict, and Disaster, with a Sequel immediately following the scene.

In any case, like much excellent writing advice, this seems simple, but it ends up being extremely powerful. Having a character with a clear purpose keeps the story moving. Step 5, showing the effects of the story's conflict on the characters, helps readers invest and identify with the characters.

Again, here are the steps to a scene:

1. *Bring actor and opposing force together*
2. *Show that one has a purpose*
3. *Show interchange or conflict*
4. *Show conclusive act*
5. *The effect. (tie your scenes together into a story.)*

THE SCIENCE FICTION FIELD

By Leigh Brackett
Originally published in the July 1944 issue of *Writer's Digest*
Winner of the 2020 Retro Hugo Award for Related Work

I am sitting here staring my typewriter in the face, trying to think how to begin this article. There's so much to be said about science-fiction. It's admittedly the screwball of the magazine family. It is also, regrettably, more or less a stepchild, inclined to be overlooked and even sneered at. Anyone who has taken the trouble to read a good science-fiction yarn, and read it honestly, knows that the field is no more worthy of contempt than the detective, adventure, western, or any other — in fact, less, since pseudo-science books lure some very bright brains indeed, and names with strings of degrees flying after like tails on so many kites.

I don't know of any field of writing that offers more opportunity to the beginning writer; to the established man who wants a change; to any writer at all who has an imagination, a little tolerance, and the desire to have fun while he works. The rate of pay compares favorably with that in any other pulp group, and there is literally no limit to the adventures you can have. If you're tired of this planet, or system, or galaxy, throw it away and build a new one. You're God, with all creation to play around in.

They say you have to be a little crazy to write stf (in the jargon of an ardent fandom, is a contraction of scientifiction and will be used therefore, if you don't mind, because stf is easier to type.) Well, maybe. But we don't think we're nuts. We think we're imaginative, and forward-looking, and even sometimes a little prophetic. Were we astonished at the

War Department releases concerning the rocket gun, the jet-propelled plane, radar, and some other things they'll only hint at darkly? We were not. We've lived around those gadgets since we cut our teeth.

Take a look at the plans for the house of the postwar future. Take a look at television, plastics, new surgery, new techniques in psychological living. All of them have been forecast, used, and re-used in the pages of the stf magazines. The brass hats already are swiping our terminology!

Maybe you're one of those people who will say, "Oh, sure, they make a few good guesses and all that, but it's still kid stuff. Nothing but a bunch of funny-looking monsters chasing around, or a Rube Goldberg machine that integrates fraldemors out of the palefranesus. Who wants that junk? An adult mind has to have something real to work on."

All right. Have you read the stories of Heinlein, De Camp, Hubbard, Leiber? The social histories of the future as they might well be written, with not one monster included. Have you read the exquisite other-world adventures of C. L. Moore, Kuttner's psychological masterpieces, the emotional "contemporary" yarn like Bradbury's "King of the Grey Spaces"? All of them as intelligent, as finally written, as searching, and a darn sight more thought-provoking than most of what you read in the top slicks.

Some of the greatest writers haven't been above writing stf. H. G. Wells, Conan Doyle, even Prime Minister Winston Churchill—so you needn't feel too snooty about it. The only measure of a man's pride in his work is the excellence of it, and the only time anyone needs to be ashamed of writing science-fiction is when he writes it badly.

I'm not saying that there isn't childish stuff written and published. There is in every field of writing you can name. But too many people judge us all by the poorer comic strips.

Why should we be apologetic when we say we write for the fantasy field? We have Williamson. We have Hamilton. We have Wellman. We had Abraham Merritt, rest his soul. Why should we apologize? God knows there are enough novels perpetrated by Grade B morons.

I will say, however, that there seems to be a special type of psychology that goes with writing stf. Not everybody can do it, which is why the field is such a wide-open market for new talent. I can cite my own case, and in talking with other writers I have discovered that it has been more or less the same with all of them.

Childhood, by and large, is a long, dull period of supervision, orders, tabus, and general pushing-around by a variety of persons vested with authority and the power to enforce same. The inevitable result is that the child escapes mentally into a dream world where he is king and things are done to his liking. He is Robin Hood, he is Blackbeard, he is Tarzan. Some of these children, like myself, discover the most thrilling, the most tantalizing and fascinating realm of all—the kingdom of the imagination.

We enjoy riding the plains with Zane Grey, but we would rather walk the dead sea-bottoms of Mars under the little racing moons. We have found forests deeper and wilder than Sherwood, with giant trees lifting to a strange sun. We have furrowed seas more mystic than the Spanish Main. We have ridden the beasts of nightmare and peered into the canyons of the Moon. We have bridled the hippogriff under Kosh-tra Belorn, and there is nowhere, nowhere we cannot go.

As we grow older, we learn to our delight that many of these adventures we have had are possible. Some day men *will* be landing on other worlds than this, and much of this world is still secret and hidden. Our concepts of space and time and mass and relativity tell us that so much is possible, so many weird and incredible things going on constantly all around us. We are fascinated now with our minds as well as with our hearts and emotions. And it does something for us.

We who live half our lives in other worlds arc never upset by anything new.

We've always known it was coming. Because we're used to thinking in terms of whole solar systems, even whole galaxies, the cautious proddings of the postwar planners toward global thinking seem rather silly. We're not too much impressed by anything, and we have reams of literature, based on actual scientific data, exploring almost every social trend, so we can hazard a fairly good guess about where every shade of thought is going to end up if it gets a chance. I'll be willing to bet that not one reader or writer of stf was among those stampeded by the famous Orson Welles broadcast. We'd all have been stampeding in the other direction—to get first look at the Marshies and then pump each other's hands delightedly while yelling, "I told you so—there is life on Mars!"

The point I'm trying to make is this— unless you have always read and loved fantasy (using the term in its broad sense), the chances are you simply haven't any taste for it, and unless you have you had better give the field a wide bye. Perhaps in no other type of writing is it as important to believe implicitly in what you are doing. Detective stories, westerns, all other types of fiction use backgrounds readily recognizable to the reader. In stf you build your own background out of the raw stuff of your creative mind, and unless you are so sure of it that you could draw a map, sketch a brief history and outline the culture of the inhabitants, nobody else is going to be sure of it either. We like our worlds, and we get a kick out of doing this. If you don't, stf is not for you. And please, for God's sake, don't think you can write down to the market. Editors have enough trouble as it is.

Having led you subtly to it, I shall now spring my second conclusion. I shall even put it in italics because I believe it so thoroughly and because it gave me my start as a professional: *There is no field of writing so well adapted to the needs of the very young writer who has not yet seen much of this world.*

Beginners are forever being told to write about life in their own back yards. But most young people are bored as hell with life in their own back yards. They've lived too much of it themselves, and it's going to take time and perspective to get the taste out of their mouths. So they try writing about Buda Pesth and Paris and the Old Manor at Trembling-on-the-Brink, and collect endless rejection slips, and become very sad characters indeed.

The weakness in this system, of course, is that a lot of people have been to Buda Pesth and Paris and the Old Manor. They know how the people there act and talk, what the streets look like, and how the cooking smells at dusk. Furthermore, because the tyro doesn't know these things, the blood of life is not in his stories, and even people who haven't been farther away from home than the corner grocery know that they are hollow and without truth.

Suppose, then, that this restless young writer decides to set one of his yarns on Mars. No one has been to Mars, at least not lately. No one can rise and scream, "Kahora doesn't look like that!" or, "That's not the way the caravans go, from Ved to the Wells of Tamboina!" All the kid needs to do is read a few non-technical books on what science knows or guesses about Mars, take what he wants, modify it to suit, and knock together his own personal Mars, on which he can do as he pleases and no kicks from anybody.

Furthermore, because there is such a wide latitude of characters to choose from, the young writer is less apt to betray a lack of knowledge about people. The more he has, of course, the better—and this is the writer's chief purpose in life, to learn about people. But he can afford to let his imagination run away with him in dealing with extra-terrestrial beings, human, semi-human, and monstrous. He will find that he loves these imaginary creatures with a peculiar and passionate devotion, because they are his own fears and hopes and desires speaking out with the voice he himself has given them.

Let's say I want to write a story about India. The closest I ever came to India was Kipling and a lone Sikh with bow-legs I pass occasionally in Pershing Square. It's obvious that in trying to handle the character of, say, a Pathan warrior, or perhaps a Hindu prince, I would fall flat on my face. Four years ago, when I sold my first yarn to *Astounding Stories,* I was doing just that with characters a lot closer to home than India. But I could take my readers into the hollow heart of a dark planet between Mercury and the Sun and introduce them to a flaming Child born of the Sun itself, and make them believe it. I understood that creature. I didn't always, or even most of the time, understand the people I passed in the street, but I understood the Sun-Child because it was an expression of my own longing for freedom, for strength—the galaxy to play with, racing the comets out on the edges of creation, drunk with the sheer immensity of space. The fact that the Sun-Child was imprisoned in a dark shell was, I suppose, symbolic of my own frustration. But we freed it, the hero and I, and I suppose that, too, was a symbol. Anyway, I got personal pleasure out of the whole thing, as well as a very nice check.

In this sense, writers of stf have an advantage over craftsmen in other fields. Frequently sheer power of imagination translated into mood, atmosphere, and unusual, compelling extra-terrestrials will carry a story otherwise undistinguished in plot and characterization.

Perhaps you like stf and want to write it, but are scared off by that word "science." You're no Ph.D., and aren't likely to be, and you are thrown into a panic of inferiority by casual references to discontinuous functions in a four-dimensional space-time grid. Well, brother, you would be surprised how many top-notch stf writers don't know any more about it than you do. That same terror of ignorance held me off, too, although I was crazy to write the stuff, until a certain young man who was already big-time material in the game confided in me that all the science he knew could be put into a quart bottle and still leave room for a fifth of Scotch. Then I began to perceive that there's a trick to it.

There are, to be sure, quite a few stf men who are brilliant, scientific minds, including professors of physics, engineers, etc. Their stories are impressively larded with advanced math and all the other super-scientific gimmicks that leave us simple souls politely dazed and gaping. I often wish I were smart like that. But I'm not, and still I get by all right and have a lot of fun doing it.

There are few editors who insist on heavy science—-John W. Campbell, Jr., of Astounding Stories being the notable example. But even Mr. Campbell will buy stories completely lacking in this regard, so long as they are well done and unusual. Also, many of his important novels are based on the human sciences—psychology, sociology, etc.—which are comprehensible to any intelligent person who is interested in them. (The beauty of the human sciences is that they're inexact, abounding in conflicting theories, and it's fairly hard to get tripped up—whereas, as I know to my sorrow, blundering around with chemistry is an invitation to disaster.)

To be sure, you must have some grounding in science. Impress this firmly in your mind: *You cannot contravene a known and accepted principle of science unless you have a logical explanation based on other known and accepted principles.* You must take into account all the basic laws of gravity, magnetism, electricity, atomic structure, astronomy, velocity, and all the rest. This requires research, and there are many non-technical books available. Inasmuch as you have to observe the same rules in any story—to avoid, for instance, glaring blunders in police procedure when doing detective stuff—this shouldn't cause any trouble. Also, it's interesting to know what goes on in the world about you.

There's a wide range of material in stf, from the frankly juvenile on up. And the readers, barring a few heavy-science fanatics, look for the same things you look for when you read—entertainment, release, an emotional punch, a stimulus to the imagination. If you can give them that, let the four-dimensional space-time grids go hang. Most of us fans skip that part anyhow, so we can get on with the story.

~

Let's take a look at the mechanics involved in putting stf on paper and collecting checks for same.

If you're an old fan, you're probably painfully aware of all the cliches. If not, I advise you to read all the stf mags you can get hold of and learn what is overdone. The mad-scientist plot is on its last legs, thank God. The dictator-who-wants-to-rule-or-destroy is getting frayed around the edges from over-use. And unless you have an especially fresh and brilliant idea for the threatened or accomplished destruction of Earth, let the poor old girl have a rest. Ed Hamilton has kicked her around enough already.

Space pirates are old stuff, and there has to be something more than blazing ray-guns and thundering rockets to pull them through. And the readers are tired of the yarn based on the super-hero and the ravishing babe (who seldom has a valid excuse for being there anyhow) who get themselves all tangled up with bug-eyed monsters on some planet, asteroid, or moon. This is the story replete with such dialogue as, "My God, look there!" and such description as, "His square jaw set grimly as he aimed his proton gun squarely into the gaping jaws of the advancing monster."

When I was trying to break into stf, the criticism was frequently made that my stories were just present-day plots jazzed up with ray-guns instead of automatics, and rockets instead of planes. Your stf plot has to be part and parcel of its time and setting. It must be integrated so that that particular episode could not have occurred under any other circumstances of locale and social conditions. You see why you have to build solid backgrounds.

For instance, my novel "*Shadow Over Mars*" which will appear soon in Startling Stories, is based on the struggle between various groups for the domination of Mars. There are the Pan-Martians, fiercely resistant to any infiltration of outlanders. There is the Terran Exploitations Company, ruthless and greedy, crushing Martian and Terran settler alike. There are the Unionists, men of both races who want to use the best of both planets to bring life back to a dying world. And, inevitably, there are the little guys of both races who just want to be let alone, to live their own lives with decency and hope. This is a situation which has occurred in pioneer America and other places, I know. But the Martians, and the obstacles faced by the characters, are peculiar unto Mars and themselves, a valid part of their own matrix.

Furthermore, the old piratical corporations here could only hope to dominate a small part of a continent. Only in the future, with interplanetary commerce and colonization, could a company possibly hope to control an entire world.

It helps a great deal if you get a broad mental picture of what the world of the future is apt to be like, taking into consideration logical developments in television, transportation, and so on. Some writers even make detailed chronological charts. Decide what your own personal planets are going to look like, and stick to it. This saves inventing whole new sets of names, natives, and conditions with each story. You'll find in reading stf that authors use the same cities and localities over and over, developing various races with individual traits and customs. If you are a reader of Brackett, for instance (and if you are a devotee of the best in stf you must, of course, be a reader of Brackett.)(If you aren't, you can quit reading this article right now, so there!), you will find references to the Low-Canals, the Jekkara spaceport, the trade-city of Kahora, the tribes of Shun and Kesh. On Venus the trade-city is Vhia. The Nahali with their scarlet eyes dance in the hot rains of the Middle Swamps, and pale giants with white hair done in intricate braids fight and laugh and sail their ships, sheathed in pearl shell, across the tideless sea. Mercury is a savage place of heat and mountain peaks that stretch up to space beyond the thin air, and the men who come from the Terran colonies of the Twilight Belt are as huge and darkly cruel as their native cliffs. All this makes for coherence in your stories, gives your readers something familiar to hang to, and it's always nice to go back and meet old friends. Let's drop in to Madame Kan's on the Jekkara Low-Canal, and drink green thil in tall glasses, and watch the little dark women dance, with the tinkling bells in their ears. Ah me! Would that I could...

Mr. Mathieu tells me to let you in on my formula, if any. Well, I've been trying to hook into other people's formulas these many, many moons, and so far I haven't been able to find one. They just look at me vaguely and say, "Well, I think of a situation or a character or a setting that interests me, and then I get a guy in an awful mess, and—well, it just sort of builds from there."

If you're a struggling newcomer, you've read all the books there are on the subject, and I'll bet you don't know much more than when you started. You read the directions intelligently and they go into your head, but they don't flow through your fingers to the typewriter keys.

And until those cold mechanical arrangements of character, complication, obstacle, suspense, and so on are translated into warm and vital beings as unconsciously as you breathe, you have not mastered the "formula." I am sadly convinced the only way to bring about this miracle is to write endlessly—to read and study and soak yourself in the stuff of other people's talents, to be sure, but most of all, to write. And write. And write.

There is a thing known as "plot sense." It is, like all the other tools of this maddening trade, an intangible. It is something developed over a period of time, absorbed from motion pictures, books, stories. You're developing this when you feel satisfied with a certain story, or feel unsatisfied with another. Most people just leave it there, but because you're a writer you'll want to know why you are pleased or displeased. Plot sense is the nameless little geek that sits on your shoulder, peering, and tells you to develop character here, or emotional reaction there, or to speed up and boot the reader in the guts on page nine. It's the monitor that keeps you from getting lost in the maze of possible futures you conjure up with the first word of your story.

Some writers never seem to get a firm grip on plot. W. R. Burnett, for instance, whom I admire immensely and who can't be beat for character and dialogue, commits sins of plotting such as ruined "*The Quick Brown Fox.*" Burnett should worry, of course, but if he had a solid sense of plot he would never have had his big fascinating menace killed off-stage by a minor character, thereby leaving the book to fall like a punctured tire. I point out Burnett because he's good enough to get by anyway, and so say that if you are a genius you, too, can do it.

Basically, the stf plot is no different from any other plot. It has to have the same elements of character, suspense, action, etc. The only difference is that in non-stf yarns you are limited by conditions already imposed by nature, history, and politics. In stf you are limited only by the conditions you yourself create, taking care to remain logically true to them.

The human characters in stf have to be as carefully drawn as people in any other field. Let Buck Rogers and Superman remain king in their own domain, and concentrate on genuine three-dimensional men and women. People in the year 3044 will love and hate and laugh and cry just as they were doing in 1944. Women will have babies, men will die for their beliefs. Their clothes, food, and entertainment will be as familiar to them as ours to us. They'll squabble over politics, rob and kill each other, moan over the younger generation, and give up safe homes on Earth to go pioneering on the frontiers of alien planets, just as our ancestors went to Oregon and California.

The guy that boots his tin kettle around the Triangle trade-routes — Earth-Venus-Mars — won't be any more a superman than the transport pilot of today. There will be heroes and scoundrels, but they will be no less human than the Colin Kellys and the John Dillingers of our time. They will be motivated by the same psychology and emotional habit-pattern that motivates you, or the guy next door. The stimuli may be different, but that's all.

The human story is the backbone of stf, say what you will about ultra-scientific gimmicks. And the farther you can stay away from steely eyes, bulging biceps, snarling ray guns, and bug-eyed monsters, the better off you will be.

Most of my own heroes are fairly hard boys, not above using their boot-heels in a scrap and giving a handsome wench one of those 40-second Bogart-type kisses. They're not invincible. They can be downed when the opposition is too tough. They're a fairly seamy bunch, because to me people who have bucked the realities of pain and hunger and fear are a lot more vital, more natural, than people well insulated by money and the inhibitions of custom.

I use women when the story calls for it. A novelet usually does. If there's no logical reason for a woman, she stays out. And this, little kiddies, brings us to the delicate subject of Sex in Science-fiction. All those under 21 please turn to next page.

There is nothing wrong with sex, in stf or out of it. To be sure, much of the sex stuff, politely termed romantic interest, is the same puerile sugar-icing crap you get in all the magazines, from *Terrible Tales* up to *For Snobs Only.* The heroine is a vision of feminine loveliness. (She usually does nothing but have tantrums, shriek, and generally gum up the action so that any normal man would let her have a stiff one to the button, but let that go.) He and she exchange a little light banter, usually at its cutest just as destruction closes in on them. They wouldn't dream of making a pass at each other. In fact, it always takes them 6,000 words to discover that they are, well, in love, and they're always just as astonished and flustered as though they'd never heard the word before.

Well, if you like that sort of thing, fine. But if you don't, I inform you happily that you can get away with practically anything as long as it's well and subtly done, and you don't try to emulate Hemingway and James Cain. This does not mean that you can become vulgar and offensive, and an affair based on sex alone, with no deeper emotional meaning, would be out of place as well as dull. But sensitive, adult. writing can put over equally adult situations. If you don't believe me, take a look at C. L. Moore's last novel for *Astounding*.

From my own work ("*Thralls of the Endless Might,*" Planet Stories, Fall, '43) here is a case in point. The setting is a lost colony of Earthmen, wrecked long ago on an asteroid far from the Sun. Generations of environment have wrought changes in them, a degenerative evolution returning slowly to the primitive. A boy and a girl are trapped, alone in a bleak wilderness, facing death.

> A strange cold terror took him. He turned his head toward the yellow girl and saw the same thing in her eyes. They looked at each other, not moving nor breathing, thinking that they were young and going to die.
>
> He shivered. The girl's golden body burned in the grey light. He moved. He didn't know why, only that he had to. He took her in his arms and found her lips and kissed them, roughly, with an urgent, painful hunger. She fought him a little and then lay still against him.

If that ain't sex, brother, I don't know what is. It is also, I think in my humble way, truth. My women are usually on the bitchy side — warm-blooded, hot-tempered, but gutty and intelligent. I like them, and I have fun working with them. I find that a great deal can be accomplished, when the temperature gets too warm, by simply slapping the space lever twice and letting the reader fill in the gap himself. Just try to be honest, not dirty, and you'll be okay.

~

Next comes the question of ideas. People are always asking me how I think up these things, and I always give them the old saw about lobster and ice cream. But seriously, happenings in the news can be translated into the future. Put Rickenbacker's raft, for instance, in a Venusian ocean and see what happens.

The stories of other writers, particularly the classics, arc fertile sources, and that doesn't mean plagiarism. Nobody can copyright a mood or an emotion. The idea for one of my favorite yarns, "*Veil of Astellar*", which will appear soon in *Thrilling Wonder Stories,* came from Lord Dunsany's tale, "*The Man with the Golden Ear-rings.*" Another of my favorites, "*The Halfling,*" which came out in *Astonishing Stories,* was inspired in part by "The Maltese Falcon" and the circus-of-the-future background just naturally grew out of Ringling Bros.

The physical properties of the worlds you create often suggest plots. I used to get my hero crashed or abandoned on page one and let him stagger off into the caves of Mercury or some place to see what he could see. The result was that Julie (Julius Schwartz, my guardian angel, sometimes spelled agent) wrote plaintively to please quit sending him so many stories beginning with just one guy going somewhere. A story, he pointed out, should have characters, plural. So let that be a lesson to you, too. Nonetheless, I still get yens to explore my private planets. A recent sale to *Planet Stories* was the result of interest in the ancient cities long buried under the warm and hungry seas.

Monsters—that is to say, creatures nonhuman and evolved under different environmental conditions—are a necessary adjunct to stf, and not to be sneered at unless they are crudely done. I always try to give my queeps and fraldemors at least a touch of beauty and sympathy. I believe in them. I know where they came from, and why, and how. I am not interested in dull masses of flesh equipped with an unlikely array of fangs, tentacles, claws, mandibles, and glaring eyeballs, usually four of them mounted on stalks. Some of these e-t's (extra-terrestrials, to you) are merely projections of our own dogs and horses and wild life. Others are your most fragile, or fascinating, or terrifying characters.

Be careful of your names, when christening people and places beyond this earth. I got a lot of complaints at first because most of mine looked like Zqfxl, which is difficult to pronounce and therefore annoying to the reader.

Well, and there it is. The trailways of space are before you, to blaze as you will. The editors of the science-fiction mags are a swell bunch—my special and personal thanks to Alden Norton, Malcolm Reiss, Scott Peacock, Leo Margulies, and Oscar Friend. All the books have felt the paper pinch badly. But on the other hand, much of their big-name, big-producer talent is in service, or busy in Washington, so the gates swing for new blood.

I'll be looking for you when I get back. Right now my little Fitts-Sothem is warming up in the launching rack, ready to blast off for Venus. There's a situation developing there, up in the high plateaus north of the Sea of Morning Opals. I've got to see what happens.

I, for one, vote we start calling it scientifiction again, and abbreviate it stf while we're at it.

Break it Up!

By Robert Leslie Bellem
Originally published in the July 1994 issue of *Writer's Digest*

Of our fraternal sins, perhaps the most glaring is triteness in dialogue. Oh brother, the things that come to editors between quotation marks! If people actually talked that way, deafness would be a blessing.

If your stories contain boring conversation, the thing to learn is best expressed in three little words:

Break it up!

Let me illustrate this point with a scene egotistically lifted from a novelette of mine, *"Murder At Auction"* which I sold to *Hollywood Detective Magazine*. The back-drop is an apartment where murder has recently been committed. The two characters on stage are John J. Horner, a studio sleuth, and his employer, Lew Quarrie, production chief of Epicure Pictures. Lew is fit to be tied because Horner has failed to do a certain job to which he was assigned, and has just finished giving Horner a tongue-lashing, Horner resents this.

Here's how it might have been written, God forbid; in which case my editor would justifiably have blown his top:

Horner was angry. "You cannot talk to me that way," he thundered. "You have browbeaten me ever since I first went to work for you, and I am getting tired of it. I am not your slave. I am no man's slave. Effective immediately, kindly accept my resignation. Good-bye."

"Please wait a minute," Quarrie implored. "I did not intend to offend you or arouse your ire. You must not resign and leave me in this dreadful predicament, which is partly your fault. I need your help, desperately. Do you remember the auction sale to which I sent you this afternoon, at which time I instructed you to purchase a list of the late Don Ballantyne's personal effects? Well, you bought everything I asked for except one article, a lacquer box full of trinkets; but that was the very object I particularly wanted."

"Then you should have informed me of your desires," Horner retorted. "I was under the impression that you merely desired a number of Ballantyne keepsakes and I had already purchased a vast quantity of them. So when some girl with black hair began bidding against me for the box and ran the price up to three hundred dollars, I decided to drop out. I took it upon myself not to spend your money for what seemed to me a collection of useless items."

"Useless items indeed!" Quarrie said in a horrified tone. "I did not tell you so at the time, but the box in question contained a large fortune in diamonds."

Who, in real life, ever talked in such a manner? Certainly, not a studio dick and his superior. As I see it, dialogue serves two purposes. First, it gives forward motion to the story; it is informative with regard to the plot. And second, it characterizes the speakers; it tags them for what they are. Therefore, since I had motion picture people on stage, not pedants, I handled the scene this way:

"Sorry," Horner said with deceptive meekness. "You mentioned a corpse?"

"Yes. I—"

"Then shove it up your nostrils. I resign."

Quarrie blocked him. "You can't do that to me. I need you!"

"You need a lesson in civility."

"Civility be damned." Quarrie then piously called on heaven to witness that he meant no offense to anyone, least of all to Horner. "Listen," he said, "this is partly your fault anyhow, so you've got to help me."

"Ah?"

"Yes. Remember that auction I sent you to attend today? The sale of Don Ballantyne's personal effects?

"Of course I remember," Horner said. "Suppose you tell me what you're getting at?"

"I'll tell you. I gave you a list of certain things I wanted you to buy in for me—"

"And I bought them. All except one."

"One!" Quarrie said in a tone of suppressed rage. "The one I really wanted."

Horner lifted a bushy red eyebrow. "A box full of trinkets and trivia? Be serious."

"Look. Those other things I told you to bid on were merely blinds. It was the lacquer box I was particular about. And its contents."

"Then you should have let me in on the secret," Horner said. (Here follows a brief allusion to the brunette girl who had outbid him.) "I couldn't see spending three centuries, even of your money, for a mass of junk."

"Junk!" Quarrie moaned, biting a fingernail and asking God to give him strength. "You call diamonds junk?"

There, you see, I have broken up the dialogue and, I hope, used it for its two principal ends: to impart forward motion and expound the plot structure, and, at the same time, to characterize the men who do the talking. It has the phonographic quality of actual speech reproduced.

~

How do real people sound when they're talking? They run words together, hastily and often sloppily according to geographical origins. Listen : you're an insurance salesman calling at the office of one Cyrus Q. Doaks. You ask the gum-chewing lassie at the switchboard if you may see him.

"I am sorry, but he is out," is definitely not the way she would give you the brushoff. She'd do it this way: "I'm sorry, but he's out." That actually sounds like a receptionist, doesn't it?

Again, though, there are exceptions. A supercilious English butler would disdain such verbal infibulations. *He* would endow each separate syllable with its own adenoidal value: "I am sorry, sir, but he is out." Dialogue is a tag, among its other uses.

I sedulously recommend to your attention a recent detective novel by a friend of mine, Norbert Davis; a book called "*Sally's In The Alley*" published by *Morrow & Co.* Bert Davis is a past master of screwball characters and equally delightful dialogue. Page after page of his opus is devoted to short, crisp speech.

Or take Cleve F. Adams, who vaulted from the pulps to *Cosmopolitan* and who has a string of successful whodunit novels to his credit. Let's open at random one of his best books, "*Sabotage*" published by *Dutton*. On pages 76-77 we have the protagonist, McBride, a private snoop, seeking an interview with a certain man.

A middle-aged woman with a face like an axe said, "This is a survey office. All our purchasing is done through—"

"Thanks," McBride said. "If I ever decide to become a salesman I'll let you know." He laid one of his cards on the counter. "I want to see Carmichael."

"*Mister* Carmichael?"

"He's just plain Carmichael to me," McBride said. He smiled suddenly. "You can call him Mister if you want to."

(Presently McBride gains access to Carmichael's private office and swaggers forward, shoving a hand at the saturnine man who sits behind a massive desk.)

"I'm McBride."

The man took the hand, shook it once, let it drop. "So what?"

"Shall we talk a little bit?"

"About what?"

"About you and me and sudden death, maybe."

Dialogue has additional usages, over and above characterization or the forward movement of your story. By means of talk placed in the mouths of your dramatis personae you can set the stage; create a feeling of time. Everybody is familiar with the old tried-and-true gambit whereby a story opens with the author's statement: It was midnight, and Joe Bloke did thus-and-so. Well, for my money that stinks. A little ingenuity, and you can accomplish the same effect with dialogue and avoid triteness. May I blushingly allude once more to this "*Murder At Auction*" novelette of mine? I just finished writing it, so it's fresh in my mind:

"John J. Horner speaking," he said indignantly into the telephone. "And if you think it's funny to call a man after midnight, I don't."

The snappy, somewhat petulant voice of Lew Quarrie came to him over the wire. "Omit the cracks. Are you dressed?"

"No, but my clothes are handy," Horner tinctured his truculence with just the proper shading of respect. "What's the jam this time?"

"Don't ask questions. Drive to this address as fast as hell will let you. I'll be waiting."

"With a load of grief, no doubt?"

"With a corpse," Quarrie said bitterly, and hung up.

There are, probably, a dozen better ways in which this could have been written. I live in constant dread that some bright new young fictioneer with sparkle in his eyes will discover some of those better ways and replace me in my entrenched markets. Maybe you'll be the one, you heel.

The primary lesson I took away was this:
*There are two main functions of dialog– to **move forward the plot**, and to **display the character of the speakers**. If there is dialog in your writing that doesn't perform both of those functions, consider fixing it, or cutting it.*

Plausibility is a Sometime Thing

By Archie Joscelyn
Originally published in the August 1945 issue of *The Writer's Monthly*

I have no proof of this, but it seems pretty certain that editors have adopted It Ain't Necessarily So for their theme song. For editors, as a class, are suspicious—they have to be—and it therefore follows that one of the biggest bugaboos the writer has to contend with is plausibility.

When we come to that word, we plunge heels over head into trouble. What is plausibility? Here I stick my neck out in trying to answer, since there can be no answer. There are the usual definitions, but they mean next to nothing. Plausibility varies with the author, with the editor, with the magazine, and, most of all, with the type of story.

Get that straight. Only when you understand it will you begin to know why the darned bugaboo bothers so much—and why it pops up its ugly head at one time, and then again, in almost similar circumstances, lays down and plays dead.

The author's part is a big one. A skilled word-slinger can handle and make seem convincing a situation which the tyro would hopelessly botch. Though often it's good writing, or reputation, that puts it over, and plausibility is lost in the process.

A good example—or a bad one, as you like—is "The Snow Witch," by Dan Cushman, in the Spring, 1945, North West Romances. It's a good story, by a good writer, but consider this sort of sloppy work, which ruins plausibility. Two men and a girl, one man a Mounted Policeman and the other his prisoner, are going down a Northern river in a canoe:

"They were bearing down on something most feared by voyagers —a huge log-jam.

Logs of every size were piled there... The heap was thirty or forty feet high, and it extended down the canyon as far as the eye could see... Tom recalled the fate of two English sportsmen who blundered to the edge of such a jam on the upper Peace two years before. Their boat had been caught in the undertow, sucked in the depths beneath the tangled logs. No one, of course, had ever seen the Englishmen again."

That's the setting for what happens, and it is well prepared.

"A sharp rock leaped from the bottom. There was no chance of avoiding it. It seemed to swing up at them like a mighty axe. Jeanne-Marie screamed. The rock smashed the canoe at the forward bulge. It tore through fabric, planking and ribs. The crumpled boat hung there... It rolled to its side and swept away. Tom caught a glimpse of the girl as she went overboard.

"Swim for the rocks!" but his voice was drowned in the roaring waters.

After fighting for hours, and traveling down-river for miles, Tom comes to the inevitable conclusion that the others have been sucked under the log jam—which is exactly what the author wants you to think. Days of searching reveal no clue. Then, more days later, and miles away, they turn up alive.

It's an old trick, but a poor one. Since there can be no logical explanation, none is given, and the reader goes on from there. But it begs the situation, and it distinctly is not plausible.

But the magazines are full of such examples. Max Brand, who was a skilled writer but frequently a careless one, wrote a book called, I believe, "The Iron Trail." In it, the foregoing ruse of not bothering to explain the unexplainable is used not once but dozens of times. A man swings on to a train, roaring past at seventy miles an hour—in the dark, and alone. Hours later, he drops off it, still at the same speed, in a lonely spot, grabs another train going north instead of west, and still the pursuing villain turns up beside him, time after time.

Those feats were not merely super-human, they are impossible, and therefore impossible to explain. But merely saying that a thing happens and going on from there does not make it plausible.

But the aspiring writer, reading such stories, is able to see how bad they are, and he argues that his screed is no worse in that respect. Which brings us to the editor.

We have abundant proof that editors will take some stories which are pretty bad messes—in some places—if they are good enough in other respects and well written. The pitfall for the beginner is that he sees the errors without detecting the general excellence of a good story, and falls into the pitfall of carelessness. Don't pattern your plausibility after stories which violate all the rules. Study, instead, the stories in the same magazine by just-average writers, who *have* to be good to sell. They're a much safer guide.

This brings us to another point that's highly important. For editors vary as all human beings do, according to their knowledge of a particular subject, or lack of knowledge, their prejudices, their likes and dislikes. And that, believe it or not, has a lot to do with plausibility.

I've had many a story rejected by Editor A on the grounds that it wasn't plausible, then had Editor B buy it without finding any fault. And Editor B rejects a story which Editor A buys. It happens every day to plenty of writers, and the point is that it depends on the editor— and the slant of the magazine.

You go, let us say, to a newsstand. You buy two Westerns, or two detective magazines. Tear off the covers. Read 'em. You declare that the contents are interchangeable, that the policies are the same. But that's only a superficial judgment. Actually, there is likely to be a big difference, in policy and slant, though the plots and the general writing may be almost the same. But the very factors which make a story plausible—and acceptable— at one market make it implausible for the other.

That is an important basic fact, hard to explain. It may be clearer if we go on to the next and most important point—not type of magazine alone, but type of story. The two elements are interlocking. And the thing which is plausible in one type of story is not at all plausible in another type.

Here's a paragraph from Jungle Stories:

"He came to within a hundred yards of the jungle glade where he had left Helene, grasped a vine while in full stride, rode the pliant liana in a soaring arc to the limb of a tree twenty feet ahead. He crouched momentarily, watching his back-trail, then went with the agility of a monkey through the interlaced branches, going as soundlessly as a drifting shadow, proceeding with a caution engendered by the events of the past day and night."

Straight Tarzan stuff—or, as the editors call it, never-never land. A pulp story in an action magazine —and perfectly plausible for the type of story and magazine, because that is the accepted thing in that type. But it wouldn't be acceptable for two minutes in a Western magazine, even if the general physical conditions were pretty much duplicated.

Or consider this, from "Mr. Meek Plays Polo," in Planet Stories. (It deals with a host of bugs—just bugs which seem always to be playing some sort of game):

Suddenly there was confusion on the board. For a moment a halfdozen of the bugs raced madly about, as if seeking the proper hole to occupy. Then, as suddenly, all movement had ceased, and in another moment, they were on the move again, orderly again, but retracing their movements, going back several plays beyond the point of confusion.

Just as one would do when one made a mistake working a mathematical problem... going back to the point of error and going on again from there.

"Well, I'll be..." Mr. Meek said.

Meek stiffened and the stylus floated out of his hand, settled softly on the rock below.

"A mathematical problem! His breath gurgled in his throat.

He knew it now! He should have known it all the time. But the mechanic had talked about the bugs playing games and so had

Hamilton. That had thrown him off.

Games! Those bugs weren't playing any game. They were solving mathematical equations!

No amount of planting, or skilled writing, would make that plausible in the average type of story. But in the particular type of magazine, it's the usual thing—and so perfectly plausible.

But now let's come down to varied types in magazines all using, supposedly, the one type of story, and see how they vary. We'll take Westerns.

Here "The Devil Sent a Texan," by Tom Roan, from 44 Western:

> "I am not asleep, Cal!" Sanity, almost terrible in itself, gripped her. "I was wide awake. It woke me with its hissing. It was Frog Eye. The awful knife was in his right hand. The head was in his left hand, held by its long, shaggy hair. I saw it, I tell you! The head with its sloping skull and the big, red, right eye staring straight at me? The left one was so small it looked like a shoe button!"

Here is a character reminiscent of the Headless Horseman—Frog Eye, who goes around, carrying his head in one hand. That's a story and a type which remind one of the foregoing from Jungle or Planet —a sort seldom found in the Westerns. Some Western editors would turn it down for that old bugaboo, plausibility.

Here's a quotation from a Zorro story in West—a type notable by its absence in most Western magazines:

> Once, Zorro slipped on the wet stones in front of the chapel, and Garcia's blade flashed over his shoulder. That was how narrowly the sergeant had missed. But Zorro sprang to his feet again, and now with his back to the torches, which bothered the sergeant until he tried to turn slightly aside.

Here is a bit from "Halfway House to Boothill," one of my own stories, from Western Story—and because of the basic situation, this was rejected by another editor as being implausible:

> There it came again, this time unmistakably from one of the coffins—the one which was supposed to be completely empty.
>
> "Let me out of here!"

The point I've been striving to illustrate is that plausibility depends almost as much on the type of story and the type of magazine as it does on other factors. And that what one editor will reject as being implausible will seem perfectly right to a brother editor of the same type of magazine.

Any writer has to learn the fundamentals of plausibility—how to achieve it by proper "planting." by keeping bis story-people in character and in tune with their environment, and so on. But those are only basic principles. It's the other differences which constantly confuse even the skilled craftsman and make life a nightmare for the tyro.

Each *type* of fiction, each magazine, each editor, has a different standard of plausibility. When you understand that, and then study those differences, you'll begin to understand how to make your stories plausible to the editors you want to hit.

It is important to know what kind of plausibility your audience will put up with, and even what they are expecting. Every genre has different rules. Some let you play with known physics, some will allow characters to act like love-struck idiot. This is where alpha/beta readers can play a huge role. If somebody reads your work, they can tell you spots where implausible action pulled them out of the story.

Hand Me That Scalpel, Nurse

By Harry Stephen Keeler
Originally published in the January 1948 issue of *Writers'
Markets and Methods*

Four ways to cut a manuscript.

It will surprise *Writers' Markets & Methods* readers, I know, but there are 4 distinct and different ways to cut a manuscript — not 1, as has hitherto been thought! Even if any thought has ever been given to the problem. I have worked out the three ways over and additional to the one commonly deemed to be universally used, and have successfully used them all.

Because of the complete lack of nomenclature in this field of construction—which one might call the field of destruction! — I have had myself to give names to the 4 methods. Here they are — with my own names. And described. The first I call

THE POTATO-EYE GOUGE METHOD

This method involves going over the manuscript meticulously, from first word to the last, a segment each day, deliberately gouging out a word here—such as a superfluous adjective or superfluous adverb—a phrase there — sometimes a repetitive sentence, now and then an entire paragraph. It is a slow way— but a 100 *per cent sure way.* There is not a script written but that you can get a full one-quarter out by this method, leaving not much impairment of style, and even a little speeding up of movement.

The second method I call

THE IGNITE THE HANDKERCHIEF, BUT SAVE THE ASHES METHOD!

This is named after the conjuring trick wherein a handkerchief, in order that it may be made to vanish, is first impregnated with an inflammable salt; at the performance, it has a match applied to it, and vanishes in a puff of flame. Except that —it always leaves about a quarter teaspoon of fine ashes to be taken care of! Well, there are always a number of chapters in every novel the sole function of each of which can be found, on some cold-blooded study, to be the conveyance to the reader of a single isolated bit of information, or to forward the plot by one single sparse plot development. Well, these chapters can be "ignited" and burned right out of the script, except that their ashes — yes, the single bit of vital information adduced by each, or the plot development it has created, must be transferred elsewhere, and given to the reader through the mouth of some character, or by a news story, or a telegram, or a radio broadcast, etc.

The third method of cutting I call

THE BY-PASS METHOD

It is based on the fact that no matter how "webby"—i.e. reticulated —a novel is, it is, in final analysis, composed of a series of "adventures" linked together and woven together. As in all adventure, elements or steps can be by-passed out, leaving the net results of that adventure unchanged. For instance: if you are going from Indianapolis to Chicago to pawn your uncle's platinum watch, and intend to stop off at Lafayette to see a blonde, and heaven knows what, again at Logansport to see a man about a Dalmatian, and again at Kankakee to visit a lunatic in the asylum there, you can—if in a hurry —just go straight from Indianapolis to Chicago on the Monon Railroad, and pawn that platinum watch. Stretches as great as 30,000 words can be by-passed right out of a manuscript by exceedingly slight plot reconstruction designed to make those stretches no longer necessary to the whole.

The fourth cutting method is radical indeed and I call it

THE SAWING-A-LADY-IN-HALF METHOD

In this method, with a gargantuan novel that has come out, say, 180,000 words when your publisher has put his foot down and said "not a confounded word beyond 90,000," you can often (but not always) bifurcate that novel around the middle, making a "phoney" ending or windup to the front half and use the second half as a sequel. The second half, of course, will have to have, (a) a new smooth lead written to. give it the opening flavor of a book, (b) a clever adroit "pickup" or resume, through some dragged-in source of all the developments that took part in Part I, and (c) an early complete demolishment of the phoney ending used on Book I, i.e. Sherlock Holmes *didn't* fall over the cliff, after all! I have done this major operation with a dozen huge novels in my day, but I warn you it's a method to use sparingly, seldom, or your readers will no longer place any credence in the stability or finality of any of your endings or outcomes!

In fact, I now use Method Number 2 exclusively, for reasons that I won't attempt to go into in this short article.

But you need not feel so confined. You have all four open to you. So don't be discouraged, ever, if your script comes out too long. You are not sunk—nor *kaput!* You can sail flyingly into port, the port being the number of words your particular publisher or editor will permit you for that piece of work.

These days, there doesn't seem to be much need for shortening adult novels. Fiction seems to just keep getting longer and longer. I, however, prefer to read stories without bloat. Here are the four methods the article suggests to shorten your work:

1. *Word-and-sentence-level edits. Replacing multi-word descriptions with stronger single words. Removing unnecessary adjectives and adverbs, etc.*
2. *Removing characters who only have a tiny role.*
3. *Skip whole scenes that are not necessary. Or perhaps are just weaker that some of the others.*
4. *Cut the book in half and publish as two books.*

Wave Those Tags

by Lester Dent
From *The Writer's 1940 Year Book*

During the past five years, Lester Dent has sold 7,000,000 words of fiction at an average price of 1 & 1/2 cents. In this article he gives some hard won information on creating characters.

This, again, is a personal opinion...

Here is my formula for creating characters to put in fiction yarns.

Now... before launching out on this character blueprint, it might be a good idea to borrow some sales-psychology and build up the thing a little. To show, in other words, that it'll work—that it is being used successfully.

Though there seems to be some wariness about admitting it, most writers apparently work to formula to a great extent. Most pulp writers have devised a sure-fire masterplot, and have been writing and selling the same yarn over and over for years. A surprising number of the slick authors seem to do the same thing. And there appears to be an inclination among editors to have their own idea of a formula for a yarn, and not buy anything that doesn't fit. They call this their groove, or the slant.

So probably the first thing to do is to try to show that stuff written to formula will sell. This might be proved by—

(Editor's Note: We can think of a better way. Here it is:

(Two years or so ago, the Writer's Digest Yearbook published on article of Dent's which gave his masterplot for a pulp fiction yarn of six thousand words. At the time, Dent was living on his schooner and hunting pirate treasure in the Caribbean Sea, and we had some difficulty getting the article—in fact, the Miami. Florida, police department cooperated by picking Dent up and dragging him to the long-distance telephone so that we could order the piece. The only instance of which we know where an author got such cooperation.

Following publication of Dent's masterplot article, the Writer's Digest received several hundred letters from new writers who had written and sold their first story to the masterplot. These results were unprecedented.

We hope this article will do as much for the characterizing problem as the masterplot thing did for the plotting problem.)

In order to write a story, it seems best to start with a plot and characters. Yams can be written without either one, but it may be a little difficult to make a living selling them.

Whether the plot comes first, or the characters, seems to be a subject for argument. One method is to build the characters, then dope out a plot in which they strut their stuff in their respective manners. The other system is to construct the plot, then manufacture characters to fit it. Possibly an argument can be avoided by saying: start out the way that seems most convenient. Professional writers make both systems work. Most of them apparently mix the two systems.

Possibly the initial step in creating a character should be:

FIND A NAME

It is very doubtful if the name is the most important step in creating a character—but it does seem to be the natural first tiling to do.

Names are convenient as handles. But it helps if the characterizing doesn't stop with merely finding a name. One of the loudest squawks from editors is that so many characters are just names being dragged through yarns.

Making the name of the character different from that of any

other actor in the story is usually a good idea. Should there be Morgans, Mermans and Murtons in the yarn, somebody may be inclined to become confused.

It may also be nice to have the name sort of express the nature of the character—convey some suggestion as to his manner, appearance, nationality, occupation, or something. This gag appears to be quite widely used.

Examples: Dashiell Hammett used a detective character named *Spade,* a hard digging instrument quite in keeping with the name... Another writer of whodunnits, Rex Stout, makes use of predatory animals as a name source —*Nero Wolfe* and *Tecumseh Fox* being two instances. A further analytical dissection of these last two names might lead to the surmise that, in the case of *Nero Wolfe,* the name *Nero* was used because it conveys the idea of a guy who is inclined to fiddle while Rome burns, which the fiction character at times apparently, although never actually, does. The name Nero might also have certain inherent leonine qualities. The *Tecumseh Fox* name might be analyzed as implying a man who was as sturdy and inscrutable as the old Indian chief, externally, while actually being as sly as a fox... Erle Stanley Gardner has had great success with a character named *Perry Mason,* although here an analysis might approach conjecture. A mason is a builder, and the word parry means to fend off; which is the way the character works— fending off numerous enemies while building his cases. (Expert Mind Reading, Park Central Hotel. One Flight Up. Ask for Lester. Advt.)

If heroes have manly names, it may help.

Taking a thesaurus and looking up words with strong, manly meanings, then improvising upon them, is a trick worth trying.

In the pulps, this approach to name-making often is obvious. Pulp hacks are guilty of characters with such names as *Click Rush* and *Mace* and *Lash.*

Names of flowers and pretty things are frequently used for the beautiful young heroine in the yam. The thesaurus could be consulted for these, too.

A reliable old gag for getting names for foreign characters is to open an atlas, look at the map of his native country and pick out a town, river, mountain or anything that has the flavor, and use that.

Villains may be made to sound like rascals by using harsh, unpleasant names. Example: Didn't Hammett use a villain named

Gutman?

A good hissy, snaky sounding name has helped make many a villain.

Telephone books can be a source of names, or of confusion.

The gag of using expressive names, while a much-used one, might possibly be overdone. The comic strips make use of it to an extreme degree, but editors of fiction magazines may prefer it tamed down a little, made more subtle.

Now... here is the next move in creating a character:

FIND AN EXTERNAL TAG

This is probably the most important step.

"*Tag*" seems to be the term generally used. It means that the character is next equipped with something that the reader can readily recognize each time the actor appears on the scene.

A simple example of an external tag for purposes of illustration, might be the one-legged old rascal in Treasure Island. The wooden leg is the thing that is remembered, hence it can be considered the tag.

External tags are peculiarities of appearance, manner, voice, clothing, hobby, etc. Incidentally, it might be wise to neglect wooden legs, because editors have a horror of cripples in yarns. This taboo against cripples is worth remembering, because it seems to be ironclad.

Tagging is reliable stuff, apparently, judging by how much is used in fiction, plays, radio, movies, books. The motion pictures usually apply a very obvious form of external tag to one or more minor characters. A supporting player in a film who goes around trying to do something— work a magic trick, (aw, come on; pick a card) for instance—throughout the picture is an example of such a tag.

If the character is a minor one in the story, it seems possible to hang on a very obvious, even numerous tag.

If the character is the lead—be careful.

Don't make the tag too goofy, although the manner of handling may have a great deal to do with whether the tag makes the character seem silly or not. But make it interesting and intriguing enough to be what it is supposed to be—a label.

As a further example of varyingly bizarre tags which are made credible, it might be convenient to return to Rex Stout and his Nero Wolfe character. The character is a tremendously fat man—which is a not-so-zany tag. But Wolfe also raises orchids, and will not be disturbed by absolutely anything when tending them. He drinks prodigious amounts of beer, which must be exactly right as to temperature. He has a ridiculous horror of any moving vehicle. He is a nut on food... which, incidentally, is not the full list of tags pasted on this character, but the job is done entertainingly. The moment Wolfe comes onto a scene, *one of the tags is waved like a flag,* so that there is no doubt about who has appeared.

That last statement is the idea.

Wave the tag. It is supposed to be an unmistakable label by which the reader can recognize the character instantly.

Frederick Nebel, in a series of good pulp yarns he once did for Black Mask, used a minor character, a cop, who ambled through the yarns devoting his time to snitching things to eat, and it was entertaining; After stepping into the slick magazines—which he did quite successfully—Nebel refined the tagging device somewhat. For example, in a recent short, he used a grandmother who devoted herself assiduously to eavesdropping, the eavesdropping being an obvious character tag.

If the tag can be used in the plot of the yarn, so much the better. The best yarns are those in which there is no deadwood, so if the tag pasted on a character should happen to be the fact that he is an amateur camera fan, it might help a great deal if the fact can be made use of in the yarn—possibly the knowledge of photographic chemistry enables him to recognize a poisonous chemical which has been used for the murder method, and thus thwart the villain.

In *Doc Savage Magazine,* a pulp, this external tagging has been utilized freely. One of the characters is always dressed in the height of sartorial perfection, the fancy clothes being his tag. Another character has one of his tags following around after him; it's a pet pig. A third uses words of the most ungodly length, jawbreakers nobody can understand, at the slightest excuse. And Doc himself has been labelled freely with typical hero tags—great size, bronzed skin, compelling flake-gold eyes, quiet manner, amazing strength, fabulous knowledge of various subjects.

The variety of available tags seems to be legion. One of the characters can hate something intensely and spend his spare time grumbling about it. Or he may have a pet peeve on at another character in the story and start a squabble at every slight opportunity.

Now... How to dig up these external tags?... This is more difficult than finding a name. Unfortunately, there is no thesaurus of character tags.

Some professional writers, in order to simplify the problem, assemble tags as they come across them and file them away on indexed cards. Biographies of famous persons can be used as source material for character tags.

Perhaps there is no better way of solving the problem except to sit in front of a typewriter and write down different possibilities until one happens along and clicks.

It may prove wise to give some thought to the character tag before deciding definitely to use it. ...That is, can it be used conveniently in the story? It's embarrassing to think up a swell, intriguing tag. then find out that the thing will not fit in at all with the plot or the action of the story.

Acquiring the habit of looking for character labels when reading published yarns may be a help. The name writers, the ones who appear issue after issue in the pulps and the slicks, appear to be the ones who use the most character tags. Why then shouldn't you?

Often more than one tag is hung on a character. There seems to be no rule against it.

But for simplicity of handling, it might prove more feasible to devise one main tag, and wave that one like a flag whenever the character moves on the scene. Then the other tags can be subordinated, and used whenever convenient.

In summary: The tag is simply something that identifies the character throughout the story. If, for instance, it should be decided to give Clancy, the cop, some foot-trouble for his tag, it might start out by having him getting a new pair of shoes near the opening of the yarn, a special pair of shoes which he knows will relieve his feet. On Clancy's next appearance, he has the shoes on, and they're wonderful. Next appearance, the shoes aren't wonderful, and they hurt like hell. Then he takes them off. Finally he winds up carrying them. And possibly in the climax he uses one of them to bean the villain. God knows hew many times that one has been used, with slight variations.

Now, the next step in making a character:

Find the Raison D'etre

This seems to be a tougher one.

But it's important.

The something inside the character isn't solid and readily grasped, as are the external tags. Abstract is probably the word to use. So an attempt to explain what goes inside may do one of three things— fail to explain anything, ball it all up, or sound asinine.

An approach to the problem can be made by going back and thinking about the character, starting at birth and following right through, so as to get the feeling of knowing just how the character happened to be a certain kind of a person.

In the pulps, seems this doesn't have to be very subtle. The hero's sister is killed by crooks, and so he turns detective and is ever-after the implacable enemy of crooks. Slight variations of this old one are run ragged in the pulps, and in a slightly refined state, again run ragged in the slicks.

The whole idea is to dope out some reason for the character acting like a hero, a villain, or whatever.

While this is being done, it may prove convenient to concoct a reason for the character carrying the external tag or tags which had been previously devised. In the pulps, the reason can be simple: Clancy, the cop, has walked a beat so long he's got flat feet, and therefore foot-trouble—and because he's walked the beat so long, he has a consuming ambition to get in the detective bureau and show up these young school-trained cops who lack the Clancy experience. This ambition is what drives Clancy to do the things he does in the yarn. Now and then somebody even dresses this one up and sells it to the slicks.

What is inside the character, his raison d'etre, seems to be highly vital. It should tie in with the motivation of the story, help furnish the reasons for things happening.

The higher the quality of the story, the more important what is inside the character, that is, what motivates him.

And the last step:

MAKE USE OF CHARACTERIZATION TRICKS IN WRITING THE STORY

Wave the tags.

It helps to introduce the hero very early—in the first paragraph, usually — and have him strut his stuff, because first impressions are the strongest. This is just about No. 1 writing rule in the pulps.

A hero may be built up by having the other characters refer to him in terms of admiration or awe. The pitfall here seems to be that the references can be made over-dramatic to the extent that the device may strike somebody as obvious and silly. Villains may be built as villains in the same fashion, by having other characters mention their dastardly nature, their previous evil deeds.

Have the hero behave like a hero when faced by trouble.

Hero should stay human, though. He can get as scared as the next guy, but his courage will carry him through.

Minor characters can also be built by having the other actors refer to them, either to their external tag, or to the kind of stuff that is inside them.

Often quite a build-up can be given a character before he or she even makes a personal appearance in the story. This device is difficult to employ successfully in shorts, but it is often used in longer pieces.

It is easy to overlook the simplest *must* of all, that of having the actors keep in character. The hero can hardly go around kicking dogs and making nasty cracks to people weaker than himself. If he makes a nasty remark to a weak and helpless person, he's a cad as far as the reader is concerned. If he stands up to the big, mean boss and makes nasty cracks, that is different.

And it goes without saying that the villain should conduct himself in a thoroughly villainous fashion. There are black villains, and half-likeable villains. The black villains never do or say anything pleasant. The half-likeable cads may be pretty good guys, but just weak. The slicks seem to prefer this type of villain, but the pulps want 'em black.

It does not seem to be a good idea to have the villain become too melodramatic in his villainy. If his badness can be spread out, if he can be kept consistently bad, the same effect may be achieved with out the chance of somebody bursting out laughing.

There are many tricks for getting character effects, but probably the best way of securing them is to wade through published material, purloin what seems good, and adapt the idea a little.

Always remembering: WAVE THAT TAG.

Very few authors have written and sold like Lester Dent. Over his career, he wrote about 175 novels. For a long stretch, he was cranking out two novels per month. At first blush, it seems like this method might produce flat characters. I suppose if you only use the three tags he suggests with never an additional descriptor, it might. Of course, if you use them right, it will serve to strengthen characters and make them more recognizable and memorable.

1. *Start with a character-establishing name. Depending on your genre, there may be a line to walk. After all, not every story can support a hero named, "Brawn E. Rippedman".*

2. *Find an external tag for the character. If you've ever read a Doc Savage book, you can tell exactly how much Dent believed in this. And it is glorious fun.*

3. *Choose a motivation that is at the core of everything the character does.*

4. *Introduce the main character(s) using 1-3. Use those names, external tags and internal tags.*

"E" Plus Motion

By Roxanne Barber Rogers
Originally published in the October 1949 issue of
Writers' Markets and Methods

"Feel what you write!"

That was the sage advice given to me several years ago by an editor, who was at the time my employer.

"To possess a thorough knowledge of a subject is, of course, of primary importance," he told me. "But it is only an outer shell, a dead body without a soul, until the writer breathes life into it with a sense of intimacy and immediacy. You've got to get that emotional punch in there."

A friend who was just sticking the point of the knife into the icing on her writing career, asked me to read a manuscript and to let her know my honest opinion of it. As I read the story, I came across tidbits such as these: -

"Two heavy plump tears splashed into her lap and made withered spots on what had been a freshly starched dress."

"A low cry of pain froze Laura's blood. Her hatred for Louise was becoming a physical sickness. Had Doctor Lackey said four drops in half a glass of water, or was it six? Laura's knees shook violently as she struggled with her conscience to remember. The wind flung open the window, and the pages of Tom's letter settled to the floor. Now, Laura knew what she must do."

This gal will make the literary grade, I thought, she understands the mechanics of emotion.

THE STORY WON'T CLICK

The grammar of a piece can be flawless, the incidents of the plot tightly woven and concisely organized and presented, the continuity smooth and perfectly timed, but the story won't click if emotion is the missing ingredient. A story is a narrative with an emotional purpose.

When someone calls a writer "a sentimental fool," it's a triumph for the writer, for a writer is at his writing-best when he's a "sentimental fool." The feeling, the very soul without which a story remains torpid, uninteresting, is emotion.

An editor has few preconceived ideas or ideals of exactly what a story must or must not be in relation to form, content or structure to be acceptable for publication. He takes each story "cold" as it comes to his desk, analyzing it impartially as to what it is in reality, and then musing over what would have made it a better story. If these two primary factors run reasonably parallel, the editor considers the piece then from a "meatier" angle. Emotional approach is usually one of the first considerations, for the editor knows that is the feature which sells a story to the reading public. Emotion motivates the action of the story, arresting the interest of the reader and providing him with a reason to go on reading.

EMOTION IN LIFE

The everyday routine of life is emotionally ruled and sentimentally controlled. The advertisements which appear in newspapers and magazines are all substantiated upon emotional appeal. An ad for reducing salts: "You lose ugly fat fast the———- way!" Designed to go to work making the stylish-stout self-conscious of her extra pounds to the point where she will be desperate to do something about them. Or this one for vitamin pills: "Are you starving your family while spending a fortune for meals?" This ad sells face cream: "Are you guilty of a dirty face? Or this:"Are sleepless nights due to acid indigestion making you a breakfast table grouch?" These advertisements all work upon the public's emotions.

A recording company issues annually new "platters" of the immortal Caruso's soul-tearing rendition of "Vesti la giubba" from

"Pagliacci." Music lovers never tire of Tschaikowsky's "None But The Lonely Heart," or "Un bel di ve-dremo" from that operatic tear-jerker "Madama Buterfly." In 1915 a glass case which had covered the Liberty Bell for thirty-seven years was removed in response to public demand to touch as well as view this symbol of freedom and democratic power. The ever-increasing popularity of the Freedom-Train as it rolled into one American city after another was prompted by the theory that humanity thrives on sentiment and emotion.

Emotion in its qualities, shades, and blends is a life-long study for a writer. He must learn to detect emotional causes, and to recognize basic settings and backgrounds. He must conquer the reasons for his characters' actions and thoughts. Emotional stimuli must be engendered so potent that the reader is swept by sentimental magic into a world created by the skill of the author in subtly weaving a pattern out of the printed words. The reader must share the writer's emotional experiences. The best way for the writer to share his emotional experiences with a reader, is for the author to assume the identity of his characters as he writes about each one. Emotional appeal is a "must" in fiction, whether it is o the slick or the pulp variety.

EMOTIONAL APPEAL

Bible stories are based primarily upon the power of emotional appeal. An outstanding example lies in the Book of Ruth: The beautiful devotion which existed between Ruth and her mother-in-law, Naomi; Ruth's self-sacrificing vows: "For whither thou goest, I will go; and where thou lodgest, I will lodge; thy people shall be my people, and thy God my God."; the tender meeting between Ruth and Boaz in the barley fields of Bethlehem. These instances possess drama and pathos, because they call to the fore human emotions. Poetry, too, is indicative of emotional appeal. Walt Whitman's "o Captain! My Captain!"; Joyce Kilmer's "Trees"; Eugene Field's "Boy Blue," are all poems that touch the heart.

How to get the medium of emotion into writing, that is the question. There are countless methods, and most writers prefer to discover their own key to an emotional level, and to stick with it. The title is a good place to begin emotional seepage. Endeavor to get a word or a combination of words which tug at the heart-strings. Titles like "The Best Years Of Our Lives"; "Alas The Heart!"; "No Son Of Mine" and "Summer On The Water," all percolate sentiment.

How to get emotion

There are limitless ways of delineating emotion with words and their arrangement. Don't say, "Tom was angry." Prove it by describing his emotions: "Tom's hands were clenched stiffly against the sides of his overcoat pockets, and his expression showed baffled fury as he stalked angrily along the boulevard." Feeling emotion and putting it into words are two distinct and separate processes. To underestimate the importance of emotion in writing, is fatal. It's the secret formula for producing what folks want to read. Emotion is the essence of moving literature.

Soul-stirring stories do not consist of complex phrases or lengthy words combined to effect a remote plot-pattern. In best sellers are found simple, everyday words, characters, settings and backgrounds. In their very simplicity, these situations demand the cooperation of the reader's imagination. Attention to small details helps to achieve emotion. The wayward curl matted to the hero's tanned forehead by the sweat of honest toil, or the homely ragdoll cherished by a child, are small details designed to arrest the reader's emotional attention. Readers, like writers, respond to likes and dislikes. It is up to the writer to "plant" emotional stimuli generously along the way as he and the reader explore the plot together.

A degree of emotion can be attained by controlling the attention of the reader to a certain factor. Physical action of any sort has an emotional basis. A middle-aged woman smiling as she tactfully arranges yellow roses in a vase, or a bride singing happily as she prepares her first dinner, such pictures mirror reflective emotion. An overlay of reality must be removed, visual details dispensed with, to uncover the deep vein of emotion.

Pitfalls to watch

Like all sure-fire formulas in writing, however, injecting emotion into a piece can have its potential pitfalls. The danger of becoming "corny" is primarily evident in this direction. It's easy to revert to time-worn cliches and obviously hackneyed expressions without realizing it. In the days of Jonathan Swift, the declaration, "She looked as if butter wouldn't melt in her mouth," was fashionably unique and acceptable. In a modern story, such observation would merit the reader's raised eyebrow, if it hadn't already encouraged the editor's, and a disgruntled "How often I've stumbled across that one!" Be emotional! But be original!

The writer must be a happy combination of many things. He must have a sympathetic nature toward others. He must be keenly observant and possess a photographic mind. He must live among all of the people, hoping with them, praying with them, laughing with them, crying with them. He must stir the reader's emotional nature; consoling, bewildering, amusing, disappointing, surprising, delighting, frightening and challenging him. Never for one moment must the reader catch the writer with his emotional guard down.

This article is a good reminder that readers read so that they can experience emotion. For some, they want to feel the thrill of a chase. Others want to feel the warmth of a romance. If your characters don't experience emotion, your readers will almost certainly not feel anything, either.

A Method for Analyzing the Short Story

By Culpeper Chunn

Originally published in the July 1923 issue of *The Writer's Monthly*

A writer must be able to look at his work from an impersonal point of view if he wishes to achieve literary excellence. Self-satisfaction makes it impossible for him to see his imperfections, and it is obvious that he cannot remedy them if he is blind or indifferent to them. But self-criticism at best is a difficult matter, and if the aspirant is to judge his work impartially he must have certain standards by which to measure his work.

A theoretical grasp on the principles of story-writing in itself is not sufficient; the novice must know how other writers apply those principles to their work before he can successfully apply them to his own. A study of the work of representative authors in the modern magazines is therefore essential, for in such work are found, in their application, the accepted standards of literary perfection.

The purposes served by such study are two in number. It helps the young writer to apprehend the elements of technique, and it gives him a first-hand knowledge of what is successful from the editorial point of view. This fact teachers have frequently pointed out, but as no methodical plan of study has been offered, the beginner finds himself at a loss as to how to proceed, for technique is elusive, and without some definite plan it is difficult to analyze a story and lay its elements bare.

The following brief plan, in the form of a series of questions, has therefore been drawn up in an attempt to meet this very obvious need. The several elements of technique, as well as other important points, have been conveniently arranged and may—and should —be studied separately.

As the primary motive of the analyst is to apply eventually to his own work the standards of the writer he is analyzing, it is necessary for him to have a thorough understanding of the manner in which various effects are created. It is therefore of importance that a story should be read several times and thoroughly digested and assimilated before an analysis is attempted. If this plan is adopted the following questions will bring out all that it is necessary to know in order to judge a story accurately.

TITLE:

Does the title rouse the curiosity and make one eager to read the story? What element gives it its power to attract? Is it suggestive of mystery? Humor? Romance? Adventure? Or what? Is it apt? Specific? If it fails to attract, find the cause. Can you think of a better one?

OPENING:

Do the first paragraphs engage the interest? Do they give frank promise of better things to come, or a mere suggestion? Does the story open with action (plot) or does the author indulge in description or philosophic or other reflection? Do you believe that the opening is as strong as it might be? Can you think of a better opening?

PLOT:

Starting Point: Does the movement of the story begin with the inciting motive or the first incident of plot development? In other words, does the author explain the motive of the story, or at once plunge into the action of it? In your opinion, is the starting point the correct one? If not, what starting point would be more effective?

Suspense: Is suspense simultaneous with the beginning of the action? Is it consistently and adequately maintained? Is there unity of effect, the unity that gives a story sustained interest? If not, can you put your finger on the weak points? Could they be remedied without wrecking the plot? How? Is the author's method for creating suspense obvious or subtle?

Incidents of Plot Development:

Are the several incidents of development introduced in their logical order? Are all of them essential to the plot? Do any of them retard rather than advance movement? Can you substitute either minor or major incidents that would be more effective than the author's? Would the story show improvement if new incidents were introduced?

Climax: Is the climax as powerful as you were led to hope that it might be? Or is it feeble? Or overdrawn? Or what? Do you feel that the author has made the most of his opportunity? How would you have handled the situation ?

Denouement: Is the solution of the problem (if there is a problem) logical? Was it unexpected, or were you able to foresee to what end the chain of incidents was leading? If so, wherein has the writer erred? -if mystification was intended.

CONCLUSION:

Is the ending satisfying or disappointing? Does it leave you glad that you read the story, or does it depress or annoy you? Can you give the reason for its effect on you? Is the ending too abrupt? Too leisurely? Does the author clear up all points that need explaining?

Can you suggest a better ending?

CHARACTERIZATION:

Are the characters clearly and sharply drawn? Are they commonplace, or are they distinctive enough to be interesting? Are they types or individuals? How are the characters portrayed? By direct description? Self-expression (dialogue)? Explanitory comment? Suggestion? Or by a combination of two or more of these methods? Is the characterization consistent?

SETTING:

Is the background or locale of the story vivid or hazy? Does it suit the characters and the action of the story? Would some other setting be just as effective? More so? How does the author work in "local color?" By description? Allusion? Suggestion? Is his method sufficiently impressive to make you visualize the shifting scenes?

ATMOSPHERE:

Is the feel of the story strong? That is, does the story seem natural -a real picture of life? Is the mood apparent? Do setting, characters, speech, dress, manners, time, etc., harmonize?

DETAILS:

Is the author's management of details skillful? Has he been too generous with them, or not generous enough? What details emphasize setting, characters, etc.? What bearing, if any, do the other details have on the plot?

VIEWPOINT:

From whose viewpoint is the story told? From the author's (with his omniscience)? From one of the character's (with his limited range of vision)? Or in the first person? Does the author adhere to the viewpoint chosen or shift from one viewpoint to another? In the latter case, do you think that he is justified in doing so? Could the story be more forcibly presented if told from a different viewpoint?

STYLE:

Is the author's mode of expression pleasing? Or is his diction awkward? Or too wordy? Or highflown? Or what? If it is attractive, what element makes it so? Clearness? Vigor? Elegance? Humor? (Effect is created by word-grouping; study of style is therefore of the highest importance.)

CLASSIFICATION:

How would you classify the story? As Psychological? Mystery? Humorous? Surprise? Adventure? "Horror?" Or what?

Has it propagandum value? Is it moral? What are its strongest as well as its weakest points?

EFFECT:

Finally, what is the general effect of the story? Do you consider it a good piece of work? If not, why not? Can you suggest improvements? Do you believe that you can lift to a higher plane any or all of the standards set by the writer? If so, why not commit the story as you think it should be written to paper? The experiment should prove interesting and instructive, especially if the two versions were submitted to a competent critic for an opinion as to their respective merits.

This is a pretty solid way to study stories you enjoy, and figure out exactly what it is you like about them. And it could be a pretty good way to edit your own pieces. Starting from this list might even be a good way to plan a story. Here are the areas again:

- *Title*
- *Opening*
- *Plot*
- *Conclusion*
- *Characterization*
- *Setting*
- *Atmosphere*
- *Details*
- *Viewpoint*
- *Style*
- *Classification*
- *Effect*

Are You a Good Salesman?

By Oliver Poole

Originally published in the November 1938 issue of
Writers' Markets and Methods

How and what do I mean by "salesmanship" in connection with this business of writing fiction? I mean just this.................everything, today, from railroads to chewing-gum and cigarettes sells only because there is terrific, high-pressure salesmanship behind it. This list of "everything from railroads to chewing-gum and cigarettes," includes stories, novels, screenplays, radio sketches—all forms of creative, imaginative writing.

Don't misunderstand me and think salesmanship-for-authors means writing letters of praise about yourself, your capabilities or the value of your stories to editors. Nor am I referring to the actual marketing of your writings—studying editorial policies, keeping up with the modern trend of literature, submitting your manuscripts to the exact markets for which they are fitted, etc. What I mean is that your salesmanship must be incorporated into the story itself; you must be able to SELL your heroine, your hero, your situations, your setting—in fact you have to sell pretty darn near everything in the story. Of course, I realize that this is an admission that the popular fiction of today has become more or less a series of colorful sales talks. Well, hasn't it?

Few of us have super-intelligent, or highly intellectual minds... very few of us. And almost none of us are geniuses. And even checking off the few who are geniuses and super-intelligent it leaves a whole herd of us who have to write for a living.

I'll try to make myself plainer. Let us say that twenty writers select a heroine called "Helene." Helene is a stenographer who works for a Wall Street brokerage firm along with fifteen other girls. What happens is, of course, that she saves the firm from utter failure and triumphs over the other girls by marrying the handsome junior partner. An old plot? You bet, old as the hills but every day in every magazine you meet old plots face to face and like them immensely. Why? Because the author SELLS them to you again and again.

We know that there are said to be only thirty-six situations, or basic plots in the writing world. That means that we have to do and re-do these thirty-six over and over again. And as over half the world writes or tries to write the competition is terrific. What puts the successful author over? Salesmanship!

~

Now out of the twenty writers who have decided upon Helene and the old Cinderella plot of the working girl who marries the millionaire, with Wall Street as a setting, one writer will click, or sell his story. Of course, all twenty may flop, but for the sake of our argument we will say that one writer sells. Why does he catch the editor's attention and win a check? Because he knows how to sell his time-worn material. It may be unconscious salesmanship but ten to one it is shrewd and very carefully planned salesmanship.

Let's investigate the story that sold.

The unsuccessful Helenes may have been "blonde, beautiful, shapely and have fairly exuded sex-appeal." They may have dressed in the latest mode but somehow they failed to catch the editor's fancy. Why? It's ten to one. again, that they were types and therefore as unreal as a fashion plate compared to a candid-camera shot. American readers are getting candid-camera minded; the pictorial weeklies have made us that way and we writers have to recognize this fact. Therefore the Helene that sold was probably a very *real* person and not at all a type.

How did the author make her real? First of all by observing stenographers very dispassionately. Maybe one stood out above the others and interested him. Figuring that if she interested him she might interest an editor he caught her unmistakeably in words and put her in his story. Maybe she wasn t beautiful, maybe she didn't know how to dress. Maybe she wasn't even shapely but thin as a rail. But. better yet, maybe she had a dryadlike grace when she walked and a grin that was so dazzling you forgot her freckles. Maybe, best of all, she had a grand and glorious sense of humor, and dictating to her or taking her for luncheon became hilarious adventures. What millionaire fed up with beautiful blondes mightn't fall for a freckle-faced red-head who was loads of fun and as graceful as a young birch tree? I'll bet on the red-head, especially if her conversation sparkled, or provoked laughter and understanding.

Or again, maybe the successful Helene looked like a young Theda Bara but wasn't. Maybe she dressed her type... tight fitting black gown, heavy costume jewelry, heavier perfume, red sandals and redder nails. Maybe the millionaire took up the challenge only to find himself facing a scared school girl -maybe this interested him?

Or maybe she looked like an angel, gold and white and sweet hut with only a dollar sign where her heart ought to be? Maybe love works a miracle but she has a hard time convincing the millionaire that she HAS a heart, or in living down her gold-digging past?

~

Of course, the modern heroine relies very little upon description for her success. It is what she says or does, how she reacts to the other characters that gives her her personality. What little description you do use must be devoid of a single fatal cliche. A cliche, in description is. as you know, the use of trite or worn out adjectives, the use of a phrase that has been done to death. For example "Helen's head was a mass of golden curls, her eyes were blue as the sky on a June morning." Does she interest you? Never! The reader has long ago exhausted any interest that such a looking heroine might have for him. What is our alternative? We might kid the timeworn description, or we might make her a super-blonde. "Helen just adored Carole Lombard! You could tell that by looking at her. Providing you stopped at her chin. Her mother bought her her clothes and they were strictly utilitarian, much to her disgust. But she knew how to open her eyes with the Lombard baby stare, and her hair, which had no need of a peroxide bottle, was towsled as Miss Lombard's usually is. You looked hard at her the first time... saw her clothes and never looked again."

Or "Whenever Tom looked at her he thought of a white kitten,

Schubert's Serenade, vanilla ice cream sodas, cream puffs, white lace fans, aquamarines and alimony. He preferred champagne and caviar. He detested cats of all kinds, and aquamarines always seemed to him like a wishy-washy gem beside an emerald ... or the white fire of a diamond. But he loved her... even while he hated her for getting under his skin with her cunning little mannerisms and the sheer feminine appeal that she exerted at each and every opportunity."

~

The motion pictures have raised Wall Street offices from dreary, useful places to highly ornate dens of chromium and glittering steel, with hanging gardens outside their windows and efficient-plus in equipment. You can do the same in your stories. Or you can give us the real, the old shabby Wall Street with its million-dollar schemes upstairs and its wistful poverty passing below in the street. The bank or this and that elbowing pitiful tenements. Bootblacks, sleek from dollar tips, carrying the most expensive shoes made as they pass in the street a man whose soles are filled with holes carefully papered with cardboard.

Or, if you don't fancy such contrasts (which are dramatic) Wall Street has a glamour all its own which you may be able to seize and put upon paper. It has a feel of money, the smell of success, of fine leathers, fine cigars, fine tweeds and gardenias. It holds the frenzy of panics, the stagnation of national inactivity, the almost insane ecstasy of achieving sudden vast wealth and the utter black despair of bitter bankruptcy. It holds the ruthlessness of power, the treachery of men to men and the golden, beautiful thing which means friendship. It is easily the most colorful street in America today and you must make the editor feel this... you must SELL him Wall Street ... at least your particular office on it.

If, during the course of the story, you resort to imagery ... it must be fresh and new ... no cliches again.

And your hero must be more than a successful, good looking young broker... there have been millions of those in stories. He should have vision, imagination and a new and different twist of personality. He might be lame and, so, left out of much that means life to most successful young brokers. As a result he has become super-astute as a financier... and, perhaps, ruthless... till he encounters the other side of his ruthlessness in the shape of his stenographer.

There are hundreds of ways of treating the old situation but if you want an editor to buy it you'll have to SELL it to him.

Written in 1938, the author says that everything that sells is sold by high-pressure salesmanship. I don't think things have changed all that much, except now the high-pressure sales is backs by enormous databases that track everything a consumer says or does. Not sure what that has to do with writing, I just thought it interesting, and a little frightening.

Anyway, I know it's a well-worn refrain by this point in the book, but writers these days may be aiming at editors, or they may be targeting readers directly, and the advice works for both. If you want to be read by a bigger-than-average audience, you need to create your own unique ways to hook the reader.

CHARACTERIZATION

By Clarke Venable
From the March 1933 Issue of *Writer's Digest*

Clear, swiftly drawn character sketches make excellent matter for beginnings. I use the word "sketch" rather than portrait for the reason that the full length picture, in all its depth and color, is developed as you proceed; the growth of that canvas and your method of handling is a high point of interest with your reader. This does not mean that you, as the author, do not know all about that character when you make your first strokes. Far from it! Indeed, only the most intimate knowledge of character will qualify you to draw those swift, clear lines that are the breath of life to this actor who, without introduction and with no need of it, walks from the wings of fancy onto the stage of seeming reality. If you do not know him quite as well as any member of your household, do not permit him on stage; he will be certain to blunder around and kick over some pet properties.

Familiar to every novelist is the question, "Do you create your characters or do you borrow them from real life?" Then if the questioner is in a complimentary mood he will add, "Your character, Lucy Nicelady, was exactly like my Aunt Hettie. I couldn't help feeling that you must have known my Aunt Hettie."

In all probability the author has known a great many Aunt Hetties. He is pleased, of course, when the readers recognize Aunt Hettie despite the thinly disguising name of Lucy Nicelady. He has rung the bell; he has done more than make his character seem real. She is real.

But to answer the question: I am slow to adopt the word "create" in connection with the development of characters. It is my honest though humble opinion that the novelist does not actually create.

It is far more probable that he makes use of what has come to hand. If he is observing (and he will never be a novelist if he is not) he has turned to some account every human experience and every human contact. He studies people. He observes and analyzes their actions and reactions. He is a student of human nature as it is, not a preacher trying to show them a better way.

In addition to all this, his mind becomes something of a portrait album.

He kodaks as he goes. The better prints—the sharp, clear-cut ones—are filed away in a manner as mysterious as it is individual with every novelist. But filed away they are, and there in the mental filing cabinet they remain, awaiting a call to the boards.

When called at last it is highly probable that the character called will not completely fill the bill of specifications and requirements. Physically, his appearance may be all right but there is more to characterization than mere physical appearance. The one called, therefore, will need a few things taken from the lives of others. More prints are drawn from the filing cabinet. They are imposed, one upon the other, and in the end one achieves a composite that fills the bill.

~

Stricktly speaking, this is not creation.

The portrayal of life, if it be a good job, is the result of experience gained through the exercise of some or all our senses. If it were possible to go outside those experiences then one could create, but would the creation be of this world? Of this life?

If it be true that man's proper study is of man (and it certainly is true so far as the novelist is concerned) then it is much safer to borrow honestly from life itself and leave "the creation of characters" to those garlic-flavored, long-haired creatures devoted to "creative art". They are found in great numbers in smelly attics and quaintly atmospheric restaurants, but rarely are they found in the public prints. Poor souls, they are forced to create. They know so little of life.

Characterization, in your novel, is your first and greatest study. They are the actors in your set up of circumstances, and they are acted upon by those same circumstances. It is not alone a question of how your character will act; there is the question as well of how he will re-act. A strong man may beat down circumstance, may work his way and his will despite heavy odds, but none the less his victory will affect his own life and the lives of his associate characters.

How well should you know your characters ? The answer is in this question: How well do you want your readers to know them? If you really succeed in bringing them to life and life to them, if you cause them to emerge from the entangling cloak of words, then you must be prepared to be companioned with them through all the weeks and months that your novel is in the making. You will get the feeling that you have known every one of them since their infancy. They will be constantly in mind. Asleep or awake you will never quite shake them. You will know how a certain one tosses her head when caught in stupidity; you will know how another bleeds inwardly from the wounds of the world though all the while hiding behind the mask of indifference. You will know what would be natural in the character, and you must have the good sense to know that the same action would be highly unnatural in another.

How, you ask, can one be sure of this naturalness? By making large drafts upon the inexhaustible bank of life. Forget all this nonsense about "creation." Borrow freely from life. After all, from what other source can you borrow?

Look around you. Your characters are at hand. If you are going to write a story of the Iowa corn country the characters to fit that story are there—and nowhere else! You can't pick them up from some other locale and transplant them. They would be foreigners, moving awkwardly through scenes unfamiliar to them. Characters are indigenous to the soil; furthermore, they are deep-rooted there. They have the flavor of their soil, and they provide much of the color of your story. They are something more than mere mouthpieces for the invented dialogue of your story. Indeed, if they are natural, and are moving in scenes familiar to them, they will provide an amazing amount of dialogue without much prompting from the author.

~

One danger confronts every author when selecting characters indigenous to his locale. It is the pitfall of accepted types and shop-worn symbolisms. Let us take some examples:

Mr. Novelist comes into my own State, Virginia, determined to recapture the romantic flavor of the Old Dominion. Without really being aware of it he is looking for the things which other novelists have used— sometimes effectively and sometimes not. He is looking for warm nights and the perfume of wisteria, cotton blossoms and the night songs of field hands, grand life in the grand houses, and overshadowing all the tall, erect Colonel whose white mustache is Havana-stained and who says "suh" at least twice in every sentence.

Now all that is very pretty. And all of it could find a proper place in a novel of yesterday. But of that picture the wisteria and the warm nights are about all that remain. The field hands no longer sing at night, being very tired and not particularly happy. The cotton fields simply aren't here any more. Those "fields of snowy white" have been abandoned to the broomsedge, riars, chicory, and pennyroyal. Many of the grand houses still remain but their walls no longer echo the music and laughter of the grand life. And the tall, erect Colonel has gone the way of all flesh. The things of yesterday no longer fit; the people of yesterday are no longer in the scene—except as they are found in tales told by oldsters at dippered ease before the warming fires of memory.

Discovering this, Mr. Novelist, if he is a beginner, may make the mistake of picturing what he thought ought to be found here. Or he may make the mistake of turning away. If he turns away he has missed a story bigger than the one he came to write. The story of change and decay. The poignant tragedy of departed glory. Get it? You are quick! Go ahead and use it if you like. Yes, it has been used before, but if that fact deters you I fear you will never write.

Several years ago John Fox, Jr. and Harold Bell Wright made American readers hill-billy conscious. They gave us tall, raw boned, always-equal-to-the-occasion hill-billies who were God's own simple noblemen. They gave us a stage type or hill man, and lesser fry have pounded out thousands of stories wherein the hill men of Fox and Wright, slightly disguised, continue to rise to peaks of manly glory.

In some distant past a writer of good seafaring stuff gave to the world the brine-encrusted red face of a double-fisted old sea captain, and since then I have met a million of them, more or less, and all of them in books. Someone, in some distant day, invented the sinister, dark, scar-marked face that we now recognize as the villian the moment he enters the scene.

Stage stuff, all of it. Must all heroes be six feet tall and paragons of virtue? Must all villians be dark and scar-faced? Must all sea captains be of the for-God, for-England and for-good-roast-beef type?

As against the danger of getting stagey in characterization, there is the virtue of common, true types. It is a part of your job to avoid the danger and embrace the virtue.

I suppose every novelist has at some time fallen into difficulties with some outstanding, strong-willed character. He brings him to life, sets him in motion, and the first thing he knows that character has stolen the show. He up-stages all other characters, he stays on stage when he ought to go off, and he comes barging in on scenes rightfully belonging to others. He is good, no doubt of it. He is too good. He delays the story, or perhaps kills it altogether. Then, instead of having a story one has a portrait.

Sooner or later this situation will confront you. It is no cause for worry if it is a portrait that you are striving to achieve. In that case, however, you must do your work well and you must make no false representations concerning it. If the portrait is strong enough the story value can be very slight. If my life depended upon it I could not recall the story that Westcott wove into David Harum. I suppose it had a story, but who cares? Westcott is dead, the story is forgotten, but David Harum lives. I would know him if I met him in Halifax; I have seen him in hundreds of small towns. If you can do a portrait of equal strength you need not worry about the story. Your central character will be the story.

There are times when secondary characters become altogether too ambitious. They develop decided tendencies to steal the stage from your principal. They get unruly, and I have known them to get out of hand. I once had one of them spoil a book for me. He was a foil, brought into being for purposes of relief and contrast. He was a clown-like fellow, full of homely phrases that seemed to ring the bell. The rascal! He stole the show. The editor that bought the story for serialization found that it ran a bit too long. Cuts were suggested. But did the editor suggest any cuts on that big buffoon? He did not! And the artist who illustrated the serial had hardly a picture in which that fellow was not present. Critics gave him more mention than I had planned and many readers followed him instead of my story.

What difference does it make, you ask? A great deal. A story (and what I thought was a big canvas) got hidden behind a good natured ox who bossed me around much as he pleased. Brought in for balance, he destroyed balance.

There must be balance in your cast. The introduction of foils and buffoons is a device as old as the art of story telling. They ought to be handled in such way as to become the spicy and aromatic sauce for the pudding, but they must not become so rich in flavor as to cover up the real pudding.

The requirements of characterization vary according to the nature and type of story. Let us take, for example, mystery and detective stories. Obviously, the author has a mystery to unravel or a crime to solve. Suspense is piled up quickly. A tangled skein is presented to the reader whose eyes are so intent upon finding the ends as to leave scant time for glances at characters who are trying to beat him to the solution.

In the crime story murder must be done at the earliest possible moment. The reader has bought it because it is a murder mystery and he will have slight patience with long character sketches. Those lines must be drawn in as the story advances at the doublequick. Characterization in the mystery and detective novel are therefore much slighter than in any other type of story. You will need all the word space that will be allowed you to unravel the mystery—if it is really a good one. A few great writers in this field have been able to pile up suspense and interest through strong and unusual characters, but the beginner who enters this highly competitive arena will do well to subordinate characters to story interest.

In almost every other type of novel, however, you can go to the limit of your skill in the development of your characters. Again let it be clearly understood that this does not mean that your book should become a portrait album. Far from it. But it does mean that you have many aids for the continual development of character, and none of them should be overlooked.

What are these aids? Certainly your set up of circumstances will provide for development, for growth, or for change and decadence, according to your requirements. Dialogue will be an ever-present hand-maiden, serving not only to further the story but actually causing the characters to present us with self portraits.

Further aids to characterization will be found in the color of your story, the atmosphere of locale, and in the action (or want of action) on your stage. Remember, action is really human experience. Your characters provide that action, but they in turn are acted upon. Some change takes place because of that action. A perfectly developed character who can go through a segment of life without any change for the better or the worse is much too God-like for me—and for all those readers who buy your book because they wish to see how others are affected by life. If you have such a character in mind, make of him a graven image and place him on a pedestal where he will be unmoved by the life that passes by.

Never forget that man's chief study is of man. And of man as he is, not as you might like to see him. Give him ideals to your heart's content; endow him as you wish with strength and will power; give him whatever measure you wish of courage, faith, and virtue, but do not lift him above or out of the humanities of this life. Even the Nazarene went up into the mountain to be tempted, perhaps for no better reason reason than to give Him a more sympathetic understanding of the frailties of man.

In the last analysis man is your subject matter. Fundamentally he does not change much. He has studied himself for ages and he knows a great deal about himself. He neither expects nor wishes a new and superman from the hands of any novelist. He is full of vanity and ego. He wishes to see more of himself, as he knows himself to be.

As a novelist that is your job; the measure of your success will depend upon how truly you can do it.

This really hits home the importance of having characters the reader can relate to. I also thought the advice at the beginning was excellent. You don't have to dump everything you know about a character on the read all at once. A sketch is fine, and then layer in more and more as you go.

Cinematic Values in Story Writing

By Bessie White Smith
From the January 1921 issue of *The Writer's Monthly*

It is well known that the written word is to educate or entertain the mind, the spoken word the ear, and the pictured word the eye. When the pictured word is added to sound the combination impresses the mind all the more, and the same is true of the picture and the written word. We pick up a paper, magazine or book and look at the illustration, and we may scan it ever so slightly, but when we come to the paragraph or sentence to which the illustration refers it arrests the mind and fixes itself —we may not remember another thing about what we have been reading, yet we are most likely to remember that.

In examining the cardinal elements in story-writing and cinematic writing, I have worked out the following illustrative method, which I think will be useful to any writer striving for cinematic value in his work.

- Human Attributes:—Motive, Feeling, Emotion.
- Cinematic Elements:—Life, Movement, Color.
- Story Elements:—Plot, Characters, Setting.

There is one other word, but I shall not write that until the end. My effort will be to show how these words are linked up, made virtually synonymous and merged into that one element which makes a story.

Cinematic value is that quality which delineates human motives, feelings and emotions by action; and can be interpreted by unspoken drama, whether comedy or tragedy.

What, then, does cinematic value do for the story? Three very essential things—it gives it life, movement and color. The writer who wishes to market his wares today, can hardly overlook the asset of any one of these three.

But how do writers best obtain these values in their stories? The general answer is by physical movement that can be dramatized. But, the writer says, the story cannot be all physical movement. Certainly not; it must have three cardinal elements, no matter for what medium it is written, magazine, stage or screen. These elements are: plot, characters and setting; and each is of equal importance. Give to each a cinematic value, and the writer has produced that quality in his work that the instructors, editors, producers and general reading public are all crying for—a dramatic story.

The three basic elements of story-writing being co-ordinate and co-equal they are not listed in order of importance, and may be examined as well by regression as by progression. Setting, then, when given cinematic value, becomes color, and is the background of the story. It should do four things, delineate character, carry along the thread of narration, act as an antagonist or obstacle, and express thought through symbolism. Thereby, it plays a part in the plot and envelops the characters.

An excellent example of the skillful use of setting is found in "The Garden of Allah," by Robert Hichens. In this story the desert plays an important part in bringing the young hero to the momentous decision which forms the plot. "The First and the Last," by John Galsworthy, is another example that well shows how setting influences the development of plot, delineates the characters and carries along the thread of narration. And I could cite dozens of others.

Now let us see how authors who use this method get cinematic value in setting: it is by the choice of words and visualization. The writer who is building his story with cinematic value in mind, must visualize every word of it; he must see the three cardinal elements, plot, characters and setting in pictures. This does not mean for the author of stories that he can write out his plot in pictures and think he has a story, for he will have none. He will not even have a scenario, because the plot cannot stand without characters and setting—and that is the mistake many student-writers are making. They are writing plots without characters and without setting, or else it is the other way around, they write character sketches without plot and with no setting—in a few instances, they write setting only.

In "The First and the Last" Mr. Galsworthy takes three pages to give the setting for one scene—but in those pages the reader looking for cinematic value will discover that he has delineated one of the principal characters and foreshadowed the plot. Every word is descriptive but description that can be visualized and put into a picture.

That the scenario writer can take those three pages and give that scene to a producer in six lines and a camera-man give it to an audience in one flash does not mean that Mr. Galsworthy could eliminate one word, and yet secure the effect that dramatized his story. It means rather that he is an artist in the choice of words, and has fully developed his picturization.

Cinema craftsmanship, as well as its kindred arts, has its limitations, and the writer today cannot well afford to be in ignorance of what they are. Decry the photoplay industry as we please, we have to face facts; and these facts are that from a toy it has grown within a score of years to the fifth largest industry of this country, and the learned minds of the day assert that it is still in its infancy. That it is affecting our literature most vitally is shown by the screening of every available magazine story and book with a cinematic value that appears. Stage plays, too, have long been used for adaptation. The director of one large producing company stated to the students of Columbia University last summer (1920) "that the hand-writing on the wall shows that authors will be able within another score of years to command the same following on the screen as they do now in print."

With this in mind then, it behooves writers to acquaint themselves with the limitations of the cinematograph as well as its possibilities. The limitations, like the possibilities, for writers, have to do with words; and in considering how to qualify for cinematic value one must gain some knowledge of the words that cannot be screened as well as the ones that can; This is too large a subject to take up at length—but examination of one example will convey some idea of how limitations may be overcome by the writer if he knows the mechanics of his art. Darkness is said to be not cinematic. The only way it can be shown on the screen is by the presence of more or less light. Observe then, how Mr. Galsworthy opens his story, "The First and the Last."

"It was a dark room at the hour before six in the evening, when just a single oil reading-lamp under its green shade let fall a dapple of light over the Turkey carpet; over the covers of books taken out of the book-shelves, and the open pages of the one selected; over the deep blue of the coffee service on the little old stool with its oriental embroidery."

It is not known that Mr. Galsworthy had ever heard or read that darkness to be screened must be indicated by the presence of light when he wrote "The First and the Last." It is probable he had in mind only time and place—yet the most casual reader cannot fail to see the picture and feel the grip of drama. In that paragraph he has set his stage, and the rest of his three pages of exposition is filled in presenting his character and foreshadowing his plot. No one reading them or witnessing the flash of the camera that shows the scene can possibly fail to feel the tragedy that must evolve out of such a man's life.

There is an old aphorism that "a man is judged by the company he keeps." He is also judged, not merely in photoplay and stories, but in real life, by his surroundings. Therefore it is readily seen what a part setting may play in putting a reader or an audience in possession of necessary facts concerning a man's character.

But all the writer's attention cannot be given to setting. The next cardinal element in story-writing is character, and that word is synonymous with movement in cinema composition. This would appear to indicate physical action only, but it does not. It indicates, rather, all the things that portray the characters and make them real men and women for the reader or the spectators. It reveals the human qualities or the inhuman ones; it makes us love their nobilities and pity their weaknesses. It makes us sympathize with their sorrows and rejoice in their happiness—it is that indescribable quality: feeling put into action. Many persons confuse feeling with action and maintain that we cannot have one without the other; but this is not true, as will readily be seen if any character of force is taken into consideration. In the lives of all forceful natures there are moments too big for words or action—they can only feel. But that feeling carries, it swings, the whole course of things, and that is why characters can be linked up with movement. Again I quote from Mr. Galsworthy:

"There are some natures so constituted that, due to be hung at ten o'clock, they play chess at eight. Such men invariably rise. They make especially good bishops, editors, judges, prime ministers, money-lenders and generals; in fact, fill with exceptional credit any position of power over their fellow men. They have spiritual cold storage, in which is preserved their nervous system. In such men there is little or none of that fluid sense and continuity of feeling known under those vague terms, speculation, poetry, philosophy. Men of facts and decision, switching imagination on and off at will, subordinating sentiment to reason .... one does not think of them when watching wind ripple over cornfields, or swallows flying." There is not one word of action in that whole paragraph, yet there are not a dozen that are not action words. They paint a picture of a man's life—they do more, they paint the picture of a class of men: and the next paragraph sets forth one of that class to portray the traits of character described, and develop the plot and carry along the thread of narration.

Plot is the third cardinal element in the co-ordinate coequal list of basic elements of the written story, and life is the corresponding word in cinematic composition. To give the plot cinematic value, therefore, it must become alive, it must be emotionalized. What is emotion? The New International Dictionary gives: "Any of the feelings of joy, grief, fear, hate, love, awe, reverence, etc.; any of the feelings aroused by pleasure or pain, activity or repose, in their various forms, or the type of consciousness characterized by such feelings." Here, then, the writer gets physical action in the story—and faces the biggest difficulty in handling cinematic value.

Physical action is shown through words and deeds; there is not much trouble about the deeds; but what about the words? A cinematic composition is supposed to have no words. True, the scenario writer is allowed a few—the subtitles; but within reasonable limitations the fewer he has of these the better, so he is told by all instructors and producers. And so also the story-writer. He must show in pictures the cleverness or subtlety of his characters; it is not enough to have them toss off bons-mots, fling innuendos, hiss curses or call down blessings. These things must be spoken in words, but they must register on the reader's mind a picture and make him see the speaker—not only see the speaker, but see every circumstance that actuated the particular words spoken or the deed portrayed.

In the words and deeds of a story the three cardinal elements, plot, characters and setting, are merged; and so we get life, movement and color. And these are the cinematic values that delineate characters, develop the plot and carry along the thread of narration. How does the writer do this? By visualizing every scene of the story and selecting only those words that can make picture-paragraphs of action.

I had two main thoughts while reading this:
1. *Do not use up too much space with description. Make it shorter and more precise.*
2. *Keep the action moving. And by action, I mean have the characters continue to make choices that push the plot forward, choices that are partially shaped by the environment.*

Horror in the Ghost Story

By Leon Mones
Originally published in the February 25, 1918 issue of *The Editor*

Lafcadio Hearn possessed an extraordinary power of creating the atmosphere of the supernatural. His power was doubtless due in part to the fact that to him "Every word had face and form and voice," and to his habit of spending "long nights reflecting about the proper shade of a word's meaning." But with Hearn, the pure technique and especially the subtle psychology of writing played a far larger part. And in this last phase, a lecture which he delivered before his classes in the University of Tokio is so suggestive, that an examination is bound to be profitable.

"All successful treatment of the ghostly or impossible," says Hearn, "must be made to correspond as much as possible with the truth of dream experience."

Every one of our dreams, he declares, is for some unexplained reason constructed according to a definite plan. Of all our dreams, the nightmare, which sometimes kills with its terror, is the most awful. Now, since the avowed object of a ghost story is to excite the greatest amount of horror and terror possible, it is to the nightmare that we must turn for an analysis of the universal dream-plan and for the very elements of the ghost story.

He then proceeds to a narrative analysis of the usual nightmare. It may be summed up as follows:

Stage 1. It begins with a kind of suspicion. You feel afraid without knowing why. You have the impression that something is acting on you from a distance, something like fascination. Feeling uneasy, you wish to escape, to get away from the influence that is making you afraid.

Then you find that it is not easy to escape. You move with great difficulty. The difficulty increases; you can not move at all. You want to cry out and you can not; you have lost your voice. You are in a state of trance,— seeing, hearing, feeling, but unable to move or speak.

Stage 2. You witness terrible and unnatural appearances. There is a darkening of the visible, sometimes a disappearance or dimming of light.

Stage 3. This is the stage of struggle. You witness impossible occurrences which bring to you extreme horror and convince you of your impotence. You may try to use a pistol or a sword or a hammer. The bullet will go a few inches then drop limply without a report. The sword will become soft, like paper. The hammer you are unable to lift. Terrible things reach out hands to touch. They may grow to the ceiling and bend themselves fantastically as they approach.

Stage 4. This is the climax of the horror. You are caught or touched. The touch is like an electric shock but unnaturally prolonged. It is not pain, but something worse than pain. In the case of the week person it may sometimes kill.

This is the dream-plan, along the lines of which the world's greatest ghost stories are constructed. Let us examine one, "The House and the Brain," by Bulwer-Lytton. This is the one declared by Hearn to be by far the greatest ghost story in English. We shall divide its main plot into stages and see how closely they correspond to the stages of the dream plan.

Stage 1. A man is sitting in a chair, with a lamp on the table beside him, and is reading Macaulay's essays. He becomes uneasy. A shadow falls upon the page. He rises and tries to call out but he cannot raise his voice above a whisper. He tries to move and he cannot stir hand or foot. The spell is upon him.

Stage 2. The lamp and the fire in the room become dimmer and dimmer. At last all the light completely vanishes and the room is in total darkness. Spectral and unnatural luminosities begin to make their appearance.

Stage 3. The phantom towers from floor to ceiling, vague and threatening.

The man attempts to use his pistol.

Stage 4. He receives a sudden shock and is rendered absolutely powerless. He sits stiff and paralyzed.

It is obvious from this skeleton outline that the above story both in its plan and material is exactly true to dream experience. The terror which a reading of it excites is intense. Its air of truth is so convincing that a famous physician once fatuously declared it to be a recital of a true experience.

Indeed, when we reflect how the most intense horror of our lives is experienced in our nightmares, we very well believe that should we plan our ghost story in accordance with the nightmare-plan its object must be realized. For we are sure to stir up associations of horror and terror.

But not only the plan should be sought in dreams but even the aesthetic elements of horror and terror. The return of dead people, sounds of terrific muffled noises, the sudden life of inanimate objects, the sudden appearance of terrible monsters, all of these elements of supernatural fiction were doubtless first experienced in dreams. Indeed if the reader will examine his own dreams he will find scores of elements which can either be used themselves or else will readily suggest others.

The writer of ghost stories will do well to ponder this. It furnishes a clew to material, plan, sequence and climax of supernatural stories. In Hearn's own words, "The terror of all great ghost stories is really the terror of the nightmare projected into waking consciousness."

This short article is a great reminder of how to shape your story for maximum emotional impact. Each story problem should get larger and larger, eliciting bigger or deeper emotions, building toward a high emotional point. In this case, Mones is shaping a ghost story, but this idea maps to romances, adventures, fantasies, almost any short story. Here's the steps one more time.

    1. Suspicion
    2. Witness the terrible and unnatural
    3. Impotent struggle against the unnatural
    4. Climax - caught or touched by evil

How to Create Plots

By Laurence D'Orsay
Originally published in the March 1933 issue of *Writer's
Digest*

We are often told that plots and stories lie all around us, waiting to be seen and written up. True enough. They are in the very air we breathe, and incidentally some darned good published fiction has been based on the germs in that air. So has a splendid book, "*Microbe Hunters,*" which every writer would do well to read.

You can't walk down the street without some plot idea coming up and punching you on the nose. Often, alas! you don't feel the blow or see your kind assailant, and neither do I. Same thing when you pick up the day's paper, which is always full of *unwritten* fiction stories as well as written news stories. You have heard that before, no doubt. Possibly you have tried to isolate the germs of some of those unwritten yarns, and found it mighty hard to do so, for the simple reason that a news story *as it stands* hardly ever contains good fiction material and development.

As we are going to try to dig some of those unwritten stories out of the paper and see how they might be written up — by you personally, if you wish — we must first get firmly in our minds the governing point that the news item is *no good to us* except as a fill-up to the imagination; as something that may suggest characters and a story problem for our minds to dwell upon and work out.

For the purposes of this article, I have gone through only three newspapers—today's and yesterday's *Los Angeles Examiner,* and this evening's copy of a local paper, the *Santa Monica Evening Outlook.* That is to say, I have taken at random the daily papers nearest to my home, making no effort at any intensive search of a number of issues, the point being that any and every issue of every newspaper has these story germs in it. From these three sheets I have cut fifteen items which suggest potential fiction stories to my mind. Probably I missed at least fifty others that might have been equally suggestive to other minds, including yours.

Limitations of space prevent my going fully into all these fifteen items and their possibilities, but some of them can be chosen and the others mentioned briefly.

~

Let us first take an advertisement. (Don't forget the advertisement columns! they are almost as full of unwritten stories as Minna Bardon's love lorn columns.)

"WANTED—100 more people with $10; each purchase 10 acres uplands of Panama, $25 per acre; terms, $1 down, $1 per month per acre..."

The ad speaks enthusiastically about climate, soil, markets, products, and so forth; but I am not giving all that, or the address, as Writer's Digest isn't interested in boosting a particular real estate proposition in Panama or elsewhere. You can take it for granted; you have read real estate ads before.

There's a story here—the story of what might happen to two young things who bought some of that land and went down to the Isthmus to raise fruit, vegetables, chickens, and rabbits for the "Spigotties," and perhaps raise hell, too, or have hell raised for them.

Suggested Plot Outline:

Wilma, young movie "bit" actress tired of Hollywood's struggles, buys land from ad. Roger, young cameraman, follows protectively, despite her remonstrances. *Reader expects they'll marry. They don't. There's the story.*

Roger distrusts these polite foreigners. Warns Wilma against them, struggling to "save" her from Don Cipriano Mercada, scion of wealthy old Spanish family. Thinks Mercada a villain of old silent picture type.

Wilma likes Mercada and other natives. Says they aren't

villainous. Changes her tune when Rosita, Mercada's sister, makes play for Roger. Must save him, as Rosita's a brunette villainess—to Wilma! Hero and heroine fail to save each other. "Villain" wins Wilma at climax; "villainess" wins Roger.

Wilma's and Roger's "back to the land" enterprises fail. That doesn't matter. Rosita suggests there's big money in making a picture themselves — exotic travelogue story. Suits Roger's ambition, already planted. But the expense?

Mercada demonstrates villainy by putting up all money he can raise. Rosita shows herself a villainess by supplying rest, having won prize in government lottery.

The title of the story might be: "*These Villainous Foreigners!*" or something like that. Start with Roger telling Wilma, Don Cipriano is a villain. The style and general treatment should be light, bright, humorous, brisk, and genially satirical. You *and your reader* should be laughing up your sleeve at your characters all the time, and yet feeling they are charming people.

If thus written, and if high in literary quality and entertainment value, this story should stand an equally good chance with any of the general fiction slicks, including the women's magazines. It should be generally slanted for them. It is impossible to "tell where it can be sold," in the sense of mentioning the likeliest market, for there is no likeliest market.

At least twenty publications are equally likely to accept such a story, if it is high in fiction interest and well written. I could easily name a magazine, but why lie? It would be no more likely to be taken by that magazine than by many others. That is true of the vast majority of the stories used by the general fiction slicks and the women's magazines, although yarns of masculine heroism or rollicking humor would not appeal to the latter as they might to *Collier's*.

In this connection, perhaps I may be allowed to quote a pertinent passage from the explanatory analysis of one of the short stories in my latest book, "*Stories You Can Sell.*" It may be heresy to the slanting hot-gospellers, but I have proved its truth in countless specific cases.

"Correspondents often ask me about the desirability of slanting for a particular market when writing 'slick paper stuff.' I reply, 'Slant generally for all of them. One is just as likely to take the yarn as another." My experience with this story bears out that belief. I wrote it with an eye to *The Saturday Evening Post,* slanting for that market if for any in particular. When I came to address the envelope, I changed my mind on a mere whim and sent the script to The *Women's Home Companion* instead. It was bought on that first trip. I was afterwards given to understand, on pretty good authority, that the Post would have taken it. This is only one of many experiences which have convinced me that you should not slant for any particular slick, or, to put it more correctly, that you cannot slant for one without also slanting for others."

Needless to say, one must slant pretty closely for a specializing pulp which only prints one kind of a story, or two or three kinds, and wants its stuff written in a certain definite way. That is a very different proposition, and the pulp slanting idea should not be dragged out of its proper place and incorrectly applied to general fiction markets which it does not suit. My own appreciation of the true slanting problem was, perhaps, proved when I slanted "*The Price of Empire*" in Writer's Digest, and sold it to *Soldiers of Fortune.*

Editor Smith and Editor Brown will each tell you, "Slant for me. Cock your eye at me only." You'll write for Smith, and he will buy instead a story written for Brown, while Brown takes yours after Smith has rejected it. So it goes.

~

Well, here's another cutting. Let's see what we can do with it.

"High ranking Navy officers were honored dinner guests last night at the Pasadena home of Adolph Schleicher, former president of the Los Angeles Chamber of Commerce."

This is just an ordinary "society note," such as one may find continually in any daily paper. The remarkable thing about it is that the list of dinner guests includes the names of no fewer than eleven admirals of the United States Navy. Two were full admirals, three vice-admirals, and six rear admirals.

Surely there ought to be some story in all those admirals getting together at a festive board and leaving the Pacific Fleet flat for a night. There couldn't have been any admirals left aboard the ships, one imagines. The late Morgan Robertson, who loved to poke fun at admirals, would have thought this just his meat.

Suppose the Japs had selected that night to make Mr. William Randolph Hearst's nightmares come true! Well, perhaps the captains, if not out to dinner also, would have done better than the admirals. Be this as it may, we don't want a fantastic story of a superstitious naval Armageddon, for that sort of thing is too hard to sell. But this plot germ of eleven admirals at one dinner might easily be built up in many ways, both humorous and dramatic. Let's try one.

Suggested Plot Outline:

Dinner has serious purpose. Naval plans to be perfected afterwards. Twelve admirals invited. Twelfth, whose presence is vital, arrives late. Explains he thought he was shadowed. Drove around to elude spy, possibly reporter. Admirals don't want their meeting known. Public might get war scare, foreign relations being touchy.

House butler once in Navy. Punished and kicked out for striking officer. Hates Navy, especially admirals. Host doesn't know record. Has plotted kidnapping of admirals with international spy, who hopes by torture to make one or two reveal plans. Will dope drinks, so they can't resist much when kidnappers arrive.

Twelfth admiral recognizes butler. Sat at court-martial. Suspicious. Telephones. Tastes liquor. Thinks maybe it's drugged. Won't let others drink. Chokes confession from butler. Spy and helpers arrive, capturing isolated house and unarmed admirals. Spy tries to force revelation of plans by horrible threats. Eleven calm and brave. Twelfth acts coward. Plays for time to save others from torture. Pretends to spill everything—not truth. Spy finally sees this.

About to torture him. Armed naval police arrive, summoned by that phone message. Mop up crooks.

"The Twelfth Admiral" naturally suggests itself as the title of this story. It might start with the anxiety of the eleven because he has not yet shown up when expected, although known to be on his way. Convincingly done, it should suit either the higher-class general fiction pulps, such as *Short Stories, Adventure, Blue Book, and Argosy,* or the general fiction slicks, such as *Collier's, Liberty,* and *Red Book,* according to the way it is written and developed. For that matter, many a story in a high-class general pulp would do for a slick, as Roy de S. Horn, the late editor of *Short Stories,* pointed out very emphatically some time ago in an article in Writer's Digest.

~

My third cutting is a pen-and-ink sketch of a herring from Ripley's *"Believe It Or Not"* syndicated feature. Beneath it are the suggestive words:

"The herring dies almost instantly when taken from the water, hence 'as dead as a herring.'"

There you are! A story that can be written in any one of a thousand variations. Somebody, to whom his or her familiar environment means everything, perishes, languishes, or shrivels up when forcibly removed from that environment by Fate or the contrivance of others. For story purposes, taking into account the selling factor of a popular happy ending, the protagonist should be in great danger of sharing the doom of the herring, but should be saved from what seems to be inevitable wreck of happiness by some unexpected move on his (or her) part. This restores him to the familiar environment, or brings its essential quality— the breath of life to him—into his new environment to cheer and sustain him. Alternatively, the person who loves the protagonist could make that decisive move and act as the saviour. In some variations of this story, the *deus ex machina* might be used, but solution of such a dramatic problem by a whim of Fate, akin to the Greeks' intervention of a god, must be very deftly arranged in order to be convincing.

Suggested Plot Outline:

Heroine born at sea. Father was skipper and owner of a schooner, aboard which she spent childhood and girlhood. At eighteen, schooner wrecked; parents drowned; poverty ; working in a city shop; feeling "dead as a herring."

She's lovely, of course. Men flock around her. One's a brilliant newspaper man, a star reporter, apparently a born city bird. Longs to marry her. She loves him, but dreads being tied to city for life. Sea calls. Wants to be free to go back. Great temptation comes. Rich man, great traveller, owning ocean-going yacht, urges her to become his wife (or mistress—take your pick.) *Make it doubtful* what she will do. At climax, when about to yield to rich tempter, a very nice chap, she finds she can't. Goes to reporter instead. He has glorious news. His paper has made him special correspondent with a roving commission to travel to all parts of the world and write up the big stories. He is off to Shanghai now. Will she come?

If I were writing the yarn, I should call it "Fish Out of Water." It could easily be made into a rather novel Cinderella, slanted for the love-story pulps or beautifully written with sparkling dialogue for the high-class women's magazines as you might prefer. Cinderella has two princes to worry over, and a *different* dramatic problem to complicate her choice. That should provide suspensive development and give you a story.

Of course, you would need to work up action and some good plot twists. I am only giving you the bare bones, the tentative suggestions, in this outline and the others. It is a sad mistake to blue print short stories in advance in all their details, anyhow; for it means a cast-iron plot, sure to squeeze all the life and spontaneity out of them. The best things in good stories come *in the actual writing,* not the advance plotting. The characters bring them to you if you leave the dear creatures free, instead of making them fight out their dramatic conflict with chains on their feet and handcuffs on their hands. That is just what you do if you force them into the rigid confines of a cast-iron plot, mapped out in advance in every piffling detail.

~

The fourth cutting is also a Cinderella, but the point of it should be that Prince Charming *gladly* gives up rank and station for love. He is democratically inclined anyhow, and not at all crazy about the old feudal things. His big job, which provides the dramatic conflict, is to persuade Cinderella that he really wants to be a man of the people instead of a man above the people. The climax and denouement of this story are given in the following AP telegram from Stolberg, Germany:

"Aristocracy was absent from the wedding of Prince Heinrich of

Stolberg and Erma Erfert, the 20-year-old daughter of a commoner, in the ancient chapel of the 700-year-old castle here today. The wedding was simple and of bourgeois character. Among the 200 guests there were none of the usual military uniforms."

This shrieks, "I'm a fiction story." But it isn't, to my mind, a good proposition for the love-story pulps, even if you made the heroine a poor American girl in Germany. They prefer the American Prince Charming. This yarn really ought to be written up as an idealistic, idyllic romance for the "quality group" or the best slicks, with fine style, setting, atmosphere, and characterization.

Plot Outline:

I should insult your intelligence if I gave more than the merest hints. Erma's parents and workman lover make trouble, for they can't believe the Prince's intentions are honorable. Erma finds it hard to believe at first. When he convinces her, another dramatic conflict develops—a more serious one. His relatives impress on her what such a marriage will mean; he will be cast out from the social circles in which he was born. Heinrich tries to convince her he doesn't give a damn, but that's hard, as she has lived in a feudal environment all her life.

Introduce an American industrial magnate. Visiting Germany, he makes a bee-line for Stolberg. Why? Because Heinrich is a wonderful chap in *his* line of industry, although an amateur scientist—a chemist, a radio research bug, or something. Moneybags wants to hire him and take him to America, which suits Heinrich and solves the problem for Erma.

Secure suspense by making the obstacles apparently insurmountable from Erma's viewpoint, and by making the reader think, without deliberately misleading him, that she will give up Heinrich and marry the workman as a great renunciation for love's sake.

~

Peggy Hopkins Joyce, "veteran wife of many millionaires and premier collector of diamonds," arrived in Los Angeles yesterday and was given a nice writeup by a smart *Examiner* reporter. She told him she wasn't interested in men at present, but only in talking pictures.

"The she suddenly shied on the depot platform," he says in his interview. "Her path was blocked by a coffin awaiting shipment, and to avoid it she completely circled the station to reach her automobile.

"'Coffins are bad luck,' said she."

There you have both a story and a title: "Coffins Are Bad Luck." Rufus King used a coffin in connection with the attempted smuggling of diamonds across the Canadian border in one of his Lieutenant Valcour murder mysteries, but he has no corner on coffins. Another writer is at liberty to use one, making his hero or his villain try to gain the end in view by playing upon the popular superstition that coffins are bad luck, so that whatever he wants to hide in the coffin and get away with will presumably be safe from curious eyes and even official ones. Whatever variation you choose—and scores are possible—the main points in this story are what the coffin contains, why it is used as a means of transport, and by what clever deduction, mistake, or trick of Fate it is opened at a moment that brings either bad luck or good luck to the protagonist involved. This protagonist might be either a living person in the coffin, trying to escape from justice or deadly enemies; or else an individual who is attempting to transport some incriminating load, such as the stolen Crown jewels or a shipment of bombs.

Suggested Plot Outline:

Public-spirited foe of powerful gang can't hang anything on them, but knows he's to be put on spot. Pretends to die. Public mourning. Takes care gang chief suspects it's pretense. "Big shot" has hard job to make his men steal coffin in which he figures chap is trying to escape, as they think "coffins are bad luck." If you write it right, reader will also think hero is in coffin. But he isn't. When gangsters open coffin, the hideous visage of an Egyptian mummy grins at them. It's a "plant" to bring the "big shot" into the open, force his hand, and make him and his men commit a crime for which, caught in a bunch red-handed, they can be sent to the penitentiary. While they are in the grip of superstitious terror, hero and police nail them.

This story might be slanted for underworld pulps, or for those higher class general adventure pulps I have mentioned. It might also do for a short short for *Collier's* or *Liberty,* if very deftly worked out to meet the terrific competition in those particular markets. One of the best short shorts Collier's ever printed was a gangster story.

~

Well, there's a poker hand of plots—five of them. The other ten suggestive cuttings cannot be covered for lack of space, but I'll tell you what they are, and you can try and figure a story from one or other of them yourself.

1. Tito Schipa, the great singer, undergoes throat operation in Hollywood Hospital. He is overjoyed, for he believes it will make him sing better than ever, adding from two to four notes to his voice range.

2. Harry Meagher, one of the "liquor barons" of Los Angeles, is found murdered at the doorway of his home. His widow says he was in the habit of carrying a big roll of money and "flashing it." She thinks that might be why he was killed.

3. Santa Monica's famous "singing cop" has discovered a better singer in a shoeblack, and has persuaded the singing teacher who helped Lawrence Tibbett reach the Metropolitan to undertake this shoeblack training.

4. Two men arrested for blackmailing "one of Washington's richest social matrons." They had threatened to reveal the fact that her destitute brother stood in a Manhattan bread line. She didn't know it. The brother inherited $200,000 and "blew it."

5. "Judge Upholds Father's Love." A Los Angeles judge ruled that a father's love is as great as that of a mother. He dismissed child-stealing charges against a broker who "stole" his six-year-old daughter from his former wife, and then took the child to clinics throughout the country to correct her poor health.

6. Ned White, the miner poet of Bisbee, Ariz., recalls memories of early days at Fort Russell, Wyo., where he was christened. When the parson called for a volunteer to be godmother, the famous Calamity Jane stepped out from the crowd and held the baby. Another "Luck of Roaring Camp" story.

7. Wayland Echols, the tenor, sang for the prisoners in San Quentin. "He says that many of the women convicts are remarkably beautiful and pitiably young."

8. Baron Wilhelm von Brincken has been pursued by two gangsters who simply won't let him alone. They robbed him of $1,200 several weeks ago. Then, probably thinking him an easy mark, they pinned a $5,000 extortion note on his back door. He ignored it. Last night a red sedan forced his car to the curb. Same

two men. The Baron cut loose with his gat. They fled. He followed, but lost them. Such is part of Hollywood life.

9. Calling for a merciless fight against "saboteurs" in the North Caucasian agricultural region, scene of the recent mass exile of peasantry, the Soviet authorities have decreed the death penalty to persons actively hindering preparatory work in spring planting.

10. Lindbergh's second baby threatened by kidnappers. Here's a morsel for a quality story. Trace the flight to fame of a young man suddenly come to great public glory. Have harm befall him through the newly gained fame and fortune. Give him public adulation and personal triumph followed by miserable tortuous experiences due to persecution by thieves or kidnappers or what not due to his renown. Make his life wretched and unhappy. Do not insert a happy ending. Give the personal reactions of the hero by "stream of consciousness" or through the omniscient author. Draw no moral. Simply paint the honest picture of a nice young man mentally gone haywire through sudden fame followed by sudden ill fortune. Don't parallel the Lindbergh case as it might prejudice the editor.

Can you see stories in those ten news items? If you think hard enough, you should.

It's even easier these days to go fishing for plot seeds. Social media gives everybody access to a wealth of misguided passion, well-meaning stupidity, and strange happenings that you can grow into good stories.

Produce-and Think!

By Frank H. Williams
Originally published in the February 1921 issue of *The Writer's Monthly*

The other day a friend of mine approached me and said: "You seem to be selling a considerable amount of stuff to trade-papers and magazines. How do you do it? I can't seem to get anything across. There was that joke for Life that I'd been thinking about for some months. I finally wrote it out and sent it in, and of course they sent it back to me. How do you get stuff over, anyhow?"

That is a rather vital question, isn't it? How does it come about that some people are able to sell stuff right along, month after month, while others sell practically nothing at all, although the first person is no more brainy and talented than the second?

To my mind the answer lies largely in this one point: The man who is always selling is always producing; the person who makes but few sales produces only a little every now and then.

Let us examine this proposition a little more carefully and see just what there is in it.

Take my friend, for instance. He declares that he is ambitious to make a success at writing. But how does he go about making such a success? He writes a little every now and then, in a dilettante, desultory fashion. Perhaps he writes one two-thousand-word story in six months, perhaps not. Perhaps he gets an idea for a joke and thinks it over for weeks before writing it. Perhaps he secures the idea for an article, but never writes it. And then when he does send in his few manuscripts and they come back to him, he feels that all editors are in a conspiracy against him and that he simply "can't break in."

But take my own case for another instance—and I'm doing so because it is only about my own case that I can speak with perfect authority. I sell constantly. Why? Because I produce constantly. And because I produce constantly and am not especially talented or brilliant I have many rejections. For example I know definitely that during a single week I have had more manuscripts returned than my friend did in six months! In one day recently eighteen manuscripts were returned to me. And yet during 1920 I received over 450 checks from over 150 different publications.

Writing is like everything else—the more you do it the better you are able to do it. The man who simply thinks about writing and does little or none of it will never get as far as the man who writes voluminously and who learns all the while he is writing.

Produce! That is the way to "make good" at writing. Do something. Don't just think about doing it but do something. Write a joke, write a story, put a story on paper. Don't put it off from day to day and week to week and month to month, and grow soured and discouraged because you are getting nowhere. Get the thing done and into the mails. Once you have your manuscript in shape for mailing it stands a chance of selling.

And think!

Whenever you write anything ask yourself if it is being written in the right way. Is your viewpoint right? Could your story be better told from the viewpoint of some other character? Would your article be more effective if it were written from the angle of the customer instead of from that of the retailer? Would your bit of verse make a better prose skit, or would your skit be more impressive in verse?

Ask yourself all these things while you are writing, and if you answer them candidly and honestly, and if you take the trouble to make the needed changes in your manuscript, you will grow immensely in ability—and in salability. The next time you start to write something you will find yourself taking the right viewpoint instinctively and putting the manuscript into the right form at once.

Think, too, of the strong points of your story and of the best way of playing up these strong points. Would it be more effective, for instance, to bring the thing you have been calling your climax into the introduction and evolving an entirely new climax for the conclusion of the story? Are you getting hazy and uninteresting in the body of the story? Are your phrases hackneyed and moth-eaten? Does your writing lack punch and, if so, how can you get the desired snap into it?

It is surprising how many faults one can find in his own work and how quickly and easily he can make real improvement in the art of writing once he starts producing and thinking about the things he produces. A single story written during the course of six months or a year may seem like a masterpiece, and may continue to seem like one for years to come if the writer never does any other writing. But the masterpiece is apt to look like a bit of drivel if the writer continues producing and thinking from month to month, and if he is candid with himself and his work.

It is surprising, too, to find how the ideas for manuscripts multiply as one produces and thinks. When a writer is turning out but little work and is working only every now and then instead of steadily, it seems like a tremendous task to think up a plot for a new story or an idea for an article. But when he is producing and thinking regularly every day of every week he finds that ideas come faster than he can make use of them. He discovers that his mind has been trained to think and that he has gotten into the habit of producing, and pretty soon he finds that the checks are coming in much faster than he had ever dared hope for.

In a recent article in the American Magazine Thomas A. Edison spoke about a quotation which he has had printed in large number and placed about his shops. This quotation is to the effect that the ordinary man would do almost anything to get out of the job of thinking.

And is it not a fact that many persons who say they are ambitious to succeed at writing would do almost anything to get out of the task of thinking, and then of producing?

There are many who will say: "I just know I could write something the editors would be glad to buy, but I never have time to write anything. And I'm SO ambitious to succeed at writing, too!"

And for every score or even every hundred of these there is probably not over one person who says to himself: "If I'm going to sell my writing I must write something. And if I'm to learn how to write things that will sell I must think hard while I write. Produce and think— that's the way for me to get ahead in writing."

And that is the thing for you to do if you want to make a success of writing—produce and think.

You need not produce a tremendous amount of stuff—it's not

the amount so much as the steadiness of your production. And you need not get brain fever thinking about stories and articles. It is not the "hardness" with which you think about writing, but the clearness and honesty with which you think about your work that gets the results.

Produce and think!

That is the way to get ahead in the writing game!

Instead of using the word "think" you could use "improve." Review your work critically, study writing, then write some more. Rinse and repeat.

Restraint-a Dangerous Virtue

By Lurton Blassingame
Originally published in the March 1933 issue of *Writer's Digest*

In the first decade of this century the man who is America's foremost stylist wrote "*The Housewife,*" In the climax of the story King Edward, grown old, discovers the loyalty of his wife, to whom he has been none too faithful. Cabell then wrote, "Now at last he understood the heart of Philippa. 'Let me live,' the king prayed; 'O Eternal Father, let me live a little while that I may make atonement!'" But when he came to revise this story for its reprinting later, the man who strives "to write perfectly of beautiful things" had learned the value of restraint. In the present edition, the king says simply, "She waddles now . . . Still, I am blessed."

Contrast the effectiveness of these two passages. In the youthful impetuosity of the first there is more than a hint of bombast and there is no originality, for other authors have had their characters cry out for a chance to make restitution. In the revised version Cabell used one fourth as many words and made them say much more. The king here is a much more clear-eyed person than the king created by the youthful writer; he sees the toll of years, the value of loyalty, the law of compromise at work in his own life.

But that, you say, is James Branch Cabell striving always to write perfectly of beautiful things while you are striving toward the lesser goal of writing pleasantly of interesting scenes, your object being, like that of the Cabell of a score of years ago, "To contribute to the best magazines, and write some wholesome entertaining books that will sell." All right, how would you like to write a book for the masses, a book that would sell a hundred thousand copies within three months?

Charles Morgan achieved such results with "*The Fountain*". He has piled emotion on top of emotion, so that women readers tell their friends, "Oh you must read Morgan's book. It is the most *beau-tiful* thing. I just cried and cried." Yet the novel is meeting with critical acclaim because the author showed the good judgement to use a certain amount of restraint and so avoid the pathos and melodrama into which the amateur would fall when handling similar material.

Let me give you an example of Morgan at his best. Baron van Leyden has always loved his step-daughter, defended her against his own children. When they accuse her of being immoral, he calls them liars, and goes to Julie to get her to deny their statements. She tells him she cannot. All his belief in the girl, his love for her, his stern principles of right and wrong are battered about by her admission. An old man, pathetic and helpless, he stands before her.

> "... I thought I knew you better than any of them and that though you were"—he picked the word—"high-spirited, still..." After a long pause he added: "You've let me down."

> "I'm sorry, Uncle Pieter."

> "What's to be done now?" he said. "I'll have to face them. There's nothing I can say." Then with a little movement toward her that was not completed: "You'll have to face them too."

> "It makes no difference to me," she said, "what they say or do or think. That's true. I'm sorry you should hate me, that's all."

> "Not hate you, child. God forbid."

> "Despise me, then. Feel that I..."

> He did not deny it, but walked across the room without looking at her and let two of his fingers rest for a moment on the keys of her clavichord.

> "Well, there's no more to be said, Julie."

And he went out.

Here is writing which piles up royalties or, in short stories, brings acceptance at bonus rates. The ordinary beginner, writing this scene, would be afraid the reader would miss the point he was making.

He would have to interrupt the scene constantly to nudge the reader and explain what he, the author, was really making the characters do; and he would make the actions and speech of the characters very dramatic to live up to this big climactic scene toward which he has been working.

Here is the way such scenes are treated in stories which come back—

> His grey head was bowed pathetically upon his old chest while tears rolled down his wrinkled cheeks. The Baron was crushed. For twenty years —since he had married Julie's mother when Julie was but three years old—he had loved this stepdaughter of his as if she were his own child. Nay, more, he had loved her better than his own children and had defended her from their attacks. Now he felt that life was meaningless since she had destroyed his belief in her.
>
> "My child, my child," he groaned, "I have always looked upon you as one of the fairest flowers of the field and now by your immoral actions you have made yourself into a stinking weed by the roadside."
>
> Julie stood before this withering attack without being able to raise her eyes because of shame. She was suffering because she had brought unhappiness to this old man who had loved her and because now she recognized the depth of her infamy. She should have known that you cannot commit a wrong and not cause unhappiness not only for yourself but for others.
>
> "I know I did wrong, Uncle!" she cried. "He pleaded with me and passion was hot within me. I fell. Forgive me, forgive me, for I know all the agony of hell."

Do you see the difference?

~

It will pay us to stop and examine this business of restraint closely. It is a blessing, but we do not want to turn it into a complex. Like fire and water, restraint is a two-edged weapon that can wound when improperly used. You have but to go to an ordinary movie and see the exaggerated emphasis given each emotion and scene to see that the ordinary American does not care for too much restraint.

A friend of mine, who has had some success in writing for the small literary magazines, decided to do a novelette for the recent *Scribner's* contest. He is one of those persons who "cannot read a pulp paper magazine" and who is determined to get away from the obvious and melodramatic. The result was a novelette which was so restrained, so subtle in its portrayal of the slight action which did occur, that when I finished reading it I had to confess frankly that I didn't know what the story was all about. I am a barbarian who has been able to get no real pleasure from James Joyce since his "*Portrait of the Artist As a Young Man*" and who suspects "*The Waste Land*" would be better if Eliot had really known what he wanted to say. But evidently there were also some barbarians doing reading for *Scribner's* for this novelette brought only a rejection slip and remains homeless.

Restraint, then, can be made to pay dividends, as any jockey who rides his horse under wraps for part of a race can tell you; but the same jockey will tell you that to keep on the wraps will have you eating the dust of those who thunder home ahead The thing for us to do is to see how and where restraint can be used profitably.

~

Let's begin with the cheaper magazines.

Naturally here we can use very little restraint since the average reader has a twelve-year old intelligence, wants strong emotions and wants them frankly portrayed. But even in the writing of melodrama restraint can be used advantageously.

Some years ago I had a plantation down South and one summer I ran a number of crews cording wood for stave-bolts in the swamp. Quarrels were not infrequent but where there were the loudest shouts, the vilest curses, there was seldom any real trouble. Then one day someone cursed Big Joe, who had been drunk the night before. I looked up in time to see the big buck come sliding, silent as a shadow, around the stacked cord wood, his eyes and mouth as red as sudden death beneath the high gleaming of the double-bitted axe. I managed to keep Big Joe from being a murderer by threatening, in a loud voice since I was afraid, to shoot him if he came on around the wood. But that experience and the few other times I have looked upon violent and purposeful action make me suspect that the hero or villain in fiction who threatens very loudly is, probably, afraid and will do nothing.

It is more thrilling and convincing for a hero to say, as Carroll John Daly's big detective has said with quiet conviction, "If you do that, I'll kill you," than to have him shout (I'm quoting now from a rejected story), "You dirty dog! If you so much as move a little finger I will fill your yellow skin so full of lead you'll tear the bottom out of the coffin they bury you in!"

There's no restraint in that last, no real thrill. I know the author is trying hard to make me get excited, or his character is afraid and is talking for effect.

Our first guide then in applying restraint is an understanding of our audience. If we are writing for an audience which, like the readers of pulp paper magazines, believe in the expressions of violent emotions, our use of restraint can be very slight and must never obscure for our readers the real value of the action and the emotions with which we are dealing.

The second rule we can remember, no matter which markets we are striving to reach, is

—In writing of the obvious emotions which readers can more or less take for granted, we do not have to go into elaborate details and explanations.

A friend was telling me the other day about his most recent sale. "I never would have put that story over", he confessed, "if I had not sold the editor other yarns so that he had enough belief in my work to read past the first two pages.

He called me in and told me for heaven's sake to use some

restraint in my opening. You see, I was writing about a boy's resentment of his mother's second marriage and I had used the first two pages to build up the boy's love for his mother. I could see, when the editor pointed it out, that this was unnecessary. The readers were willing to admit that youngsters of ten care for their mothers; and all I had to do was to show in the story how this affection worked out."

A very good example of this is found in John Fante's "*First Communion*" in last month's *American Mercury*. The hero, a boy of nine, is supposed to wear a white shirt for his first communion. He does not have such a shirt and, his mother being in the hospital, his grandmother dressed him in one of his father's shirts. The garment flows off him so that the other children titter. The nun tells the boy to go home and get the shirt fixed before he receives communion. Instead of going back to his grandmother, the boy turns instinctively to his own mother and races to the hospital, getting there just as his mother is being wheeled from her room to the operating room.

> I saw my mother. She was too white to sew. She looked as if her face was covered with talcum; like a girl, she had her hair in a braid.
>
> She saw me. She took my hand and smiled.
>
> "He's an angel," my mother said to the nurse. "He went to Communion for me this morning. That's why I'm not afraid."
>
> I blurted: "I never went yet, Ma."
>
> She didn't hear. I half-repeated it, but the nurse pasted a funny-smelling hand over my mouth. They pulled my mother away.
>
> I followed them down the rubbery, smelly corridor. The bed on wheels swung quietly into the operating-room. My mother saw me in the hall. She asked the nurses to stop. She waved her fingers to me. I ran tiptoe to her side.
>
> "Isn't that Papa's shirt?" she asked.

"Yeah," I said.

"Let me fix it."

"You can't now," the nurse said. "The doctor's waiting."

"Just a safety pin," my mother said.

The nurse gave her one. She pinned it at the elbow of torn sleeve, to prevent any further ripping.

The moving emotion of this passage is enhanced by its restraint. Mr. Fante does not stop and nudge the reader, explaining for a paragraph that the boy knew his mother loved him and always would do what she could to help him. He does not take time to tell us that even in this crisis in her life, the mother was devoted to her son and thought first of his happiness. The relationship of mother and son is so well known that we understand the motions which create the scene we look upon.

In contrast to this, we do not know the attitude of the nine-year old from a poor section of the city toward his first communion. Here the restraint shown in the scene between the mother and the boy is not possible and the details of the emotion must be more fully and carefully portrayed.

How, then, are we to use restraint in big dramatic scenes where the emotions are not so obvious that they will be accepted by all the readers?

For an answer to this, let's go back to "*The Fountain*". The excerpt previously quoted will not, in this isolated form, bring tears to the readers who cried over it in the book. Torn from the context, restraint robs it of power. But in the book it was effective because the preceding action had built up beautifully and clearly a picture of the Baron's love for this step-daughter and his aristocratic adherence to a code of morals which Julie violates.

We can state our rule then, something like this—

Restraint is effective in the climaxes of stories in direct proportion to the clarity with which the issues involved have been built up before the climactic scene.

Let's take an example from the recent work of the man who, year after year with amazing persistence, is represented in one or more of the anthologies of best stories. In *"Will and Bill"* Wilber Daniel Steele uses the Dr. Jeykll and Mr. Hyde theme to create a beautiful story for *Ladies' Home Journal.* The Sheriff's daughter, at the age when fairies lurk under almost every tree, is captured by a band of desperados whose leader is Bill, but she is saved by a person who appears so suddenly she does not see him come, a person who looks just like Bill except that he smiles and is good to her and his name is Will.

He is, she learns, the twin of the bad brother Bill, and she comes to love him as only a lovely child can love a stranger who helps her and understands her. Elizabeth does not know that Will and Bill are two aspects of the same person and when her father discovers the gang and shoots it out with them she is desperately afraid that her friend Will has been hurt.

She is so hysterical in her demand to know that Will is not hurt that her puzzled father let's her see the dying man. And seeing him, with only suffering on his face, she is not sure who he is. Here is Steel's climax:

> The doctor bent and said to him: "Hearn! Hear me? Bill!" Not a stir.

> Down by the doctor, on the floor, she tried. "Bill! Bill!"

> "Then in misery, *Will?"*

> The eye lids fluttered. The full flesh awoke. Elizabeth felt the awful truth of the blunder father and fate had committed beginning to come at her. As if she could stop it—stop fire by pouring oil. "Oh, *don't* be Will!" she wailed.

> Of course, it couldn't have been the wail. She knew afterward it must have been just—just something. But with that, in the instant, there commenced a labor on the face before her. A battle of will against weakness so nearly drawn, it seemed but one muscle at a time could carry it on.

> Crease by crease, painfully, piecemeal, till on the brow the scowl

was finished at last. One lid, then very slowly the other, hardening to make a slit at last of the eye between them. And at very last, and very, very slowly, still it seemed the heart in Elizabeth's throat would smother her before certainty could be quite certain, the mouth straightening, the lips thinning till there could be no doubt of it ever, they were as thin as murder.

Then, and then only, they opened to a bloody, whispery, heavenly snarl:

"Will? Will to hell! Me-I'm—Bill."

"Elizabeth could let her breath go then."

Here is an excellent popular ending. Drama is here, with sympathy, surprise; all portrayed through action and with a moderate restraint. Steele is too clever a craftsman to carry his emphasis a step further than he has done. He does not stop his story to whisper, "Elizabeth was facing the first great tragedy of her young life." Nor does he try to enhance his climax by shouting, "The little girl felt as if her heart would break. Vague terror possessed her! Could it be that a person she had loved had been shot by her father? Was the world so blind and cruel as to kill a man who knew about fairies and loved his mother? Oh no!"

For the whispering is unnecessary and the shouting would but drown the misery in Elizabeth's voice when, stooping, she whispers "Will ?" The whispering and the shouting have been taken care of through the building of the story as, step by step, Steele wrought for the climax. The love of the child for the man who, like Shakespeare's toad, wears yet a perfect jewel in his head; the affection of the man for the girl—all this is worked up in advance so that in the climax restraint will enhance the drama of the man giving his last ounce of strength to make the child hate him, and so be happy.

~

One of the most effective story endings I remember was but a sentence or two in length:—A young man goes out of a door; and as he passes, we see that his head and shoulders sag like those of the very old man.

Restraint could go no further. We are not told that the man is suffering; we only see him going out. But the story had built up the hope with which he entered that room, the struggle which he had put into the things he brought there and which were to give him success in the conference. We knew that he had put the best of himself in the preparation for this hour. And so, when the person he interviews says "No" we need only that picture, in a sentence, of the man going out the door.

Whether you are writing for art or money, you need restraint among your tools. But remember it is two-edged. With it you can pare out of your stories verbosity, pathos, melodrama, and other ills; but if you pare too deeply, you will cut a vein and the stories will die of anemia. Use this tool, like your others, carefully.

Knowing who you are writing for helps immensely when deciding when to restrain and when to expound. And when you do restrain, it helps build the emotion if the restraint is in contrast to something that came before or at least was set up.

The Angle of Narration

By Culpeper Chunn
Originally published in the May 1923 issue of *The Writer's Monthly*

"Why do editors kick so against a shift of viewpoint in a story?" asked a writer-friend of me the other day. "What difference does it make, so long as you have a red-blooded story? Some time ago I submitted a story to a magazine and the editor promptly returned it, saying that he liked the plot but was prejudiced against the style of work he termed "a story within a story."

"In order to develop the plot I had found it necessary to shift the viewpoint or angle of narration, and the editor contended that the work contained two or more minor stories instead of a continuity of action. The story is one of the strongest I ever wrote; yet, because of the break in the angle of narration, it has been rejected by seven magazines. Why? I have had the same thing happen to me before, and while I intend to pass up such stories in the future, I should like to know why editors have put a ban upon them."

"Have you read 'The Golden Scorpion,' by Sax Rohmer?" I asked, naming the first story-within-a-story novel that occurred to me.

My friend said that he had, and added that he thought it was a good story. I agreed with him, and then continued: "You will recall that the first and third parts of this story are told from the author's angle and the second part in the first person by Gaston Max, one of the characters. Now after working up your interest to a high pitch in the first part, cannot you recollect the distinct feeling of disappointment that came over you when, in the second part, the author dropped the main issue and dashed cold water in your face, so to speak, by attacking the story from an entirely different viewpoint, which made it necessary for you to wade through a chapter or two of re-hash before your interest would reassert itself? If you can, then you will have put your finger on the chink in the armor of work containing a shift of viewpoint."

My friend now saw the matter in its true light and was rather astonished that the point had hitherto escaped him. Like most young writers, he was so wrapped up in his work that he had been blind to its most glaring defect. When the fault was pointed out in the work of another writer he was able to see and judge it impersonally and accurately.

The foregoing incident is cited because it seems to bring out more or less clearly the reason for the almost universal prejudice against the story-within-a-story type of fiction. Indeed, the shifting of viewpoints, which results in two or more minor stories in a single work, is one of the chief complaints that the czars of the editorial sanctums have to make against the floods of unsolicited manuscripts that daily reach their desks. The matter is therefore one that deserves the serious attention not only of the tyro but also of the busy professional writer who is sometimes prone to follow the line of least resistance.

There are several approved methods of writing a story, viz: from the angle of the author, from the viewpoint of one of the characters, and in the first person. Before going more fully into the shifting of angles, let us examine into these different viewpoints and search out the advantages and disadvantages of each.

The author's angle of narration is unquestionably the most widely used of the three viewpoints. With his granted omniscience, few restrictions are placed on the writer who adopts the author's angle; he can flash from scene to scene without embarrassment, toy with a dozen situations in as many different places at the same time, probe the minds and reveal the secrets of all of his characters, and do a score of other things that it would be impossible for him to do if he were writing in the first person or from the viewpoint of a single character. Nothing is hidden from him; he has access to the hearts and minds of all of his characters, and it only remains for him with an inspirational touch to set down what he sees.

Most of the novels of the masters are written from the angle of the author. "The Three Musketeers" and "The Count of Monte Cristo" are two such stories. In fact, of all Alexandre Dumas' eighty or more novels, I cannot recall a single story that is told from any viewpoint but the author's.

The same is true of most of the short-story classics. Maupassant and Poe almost invariably wrote from the author's angle; and, if one may judge by their work, a great majority of the present-day fictionists seem to think that what was good enough for the masters is good enough for them. I feel safe in saying, therefore, that the tyro will seldom err if he chooses the author's viewpoint when in doubt.

There are many writers, however, who prefer to write from the viewpoint of one of their characters, and there is no doubt but that a story can be given a more intimate touch when written from this angle than when written from the angle of the author. This is especially true of character, psychological and mood stories, in which the reader's attention is directed upon a single character. If unity and the personal note are absent in stories such as these, interest is reduced to the minimum.

A good example of the mood story is found in "Innocence," by Rose Wilder Lane. This story, which appeared in Harper's is told from the angle of Mary Alice, the principal character, and the result is a psychological and emotional study of intimacy, delicacy and charm. Had the story been written from the angle of the author, the delightful atmosphere of innocent childhood that Miss Lane has succeeded in creating, and the cohesion of the various and sometimes difficult plot-situations, would have been absent.

Another but wholly different story worth considering in this connection is "All For Mary," which was published in a recent issue of True Stories. This character story is told in such a way that the reader assumes the part of the principal character and lives over his struggles and triumphs with him. In the latter part of the story the anonymous author introduces a brief history of Mary Louise, the heroine. But instead of shifting from the viewpoint of Warren Carmody, from whose angle the story is told, the author deftly brings out all necessary information in a bit of dialogue between the hero and the heroine. Had the angle of narration been broken, the effect, found in the unity and cohesion of the story, would have been lost.

The viewpoint of a single character, however, is not without disadvantages. After he has selected the character from whose angle he intends to write his story, the writer must stay within the range of that character's vision. He cannot look into the minds of his other characters, although he is at liberty to set down what they seem to think. He can deduce much, but directly reveal only facts within the certain knowledge of the character from whose angle he is writing.

The same restrictions are placed on the author when he writes in the first person. The story must be kept within the bounds of the narrator's personal experience and knowledge. He can look into his own mind and depict his own mental conflicts, but he may depict those of others only by inference. For example, an author writing in the first person might be sure of his ground if he began a story with "The girl approached me with a smile on her face," but it would be obviously absurd for him to add: "She was thinking how handsome I was, and wondering if I would take her to dinner." On the other hand, it would be perfectly proper for him to say, "On her face was a look of admiration. She raised her eyes appealingly, as I entered the restaurant, as if she hoped I would ask her to dinner." Obstacles such as this can easily be overcome by the writer with an adept pen.

Because of the restrictions placed on them, however, some authors find it difficult to write in the first person, and there is no reason why they should force themselves to adopt this viewpoint, as there are few stories that cannot be told from one of the other angles. Besides, it has frequently been said that a story written in the first person is difficult to sell. But this is simply a matter of opinion, which facts do not support. Maximilian Foster wrote "The Bucket Boob" in the first person and sold it to the Saturday Evening Post, one of the most difficult markets in the world. The same magazine bought and published "J. Poindexter, Colored," a novel by Irvin S. Cobb. This story is written in the first person from the angle of Jeff, the principal character.

A recent issue of Scribner's, another very difficult market, contained two stories written in the first person, namely, "The Ethics of Nelson Cole," by Charles Belmont Davis, and "The Reverend James E. Markison," by Edward Carrington Venable. These are not exceptional cases; other magazines as exacting as the Saturday Evening Post and Scribner's frequently buy stories written in the first person. Personally, I believe that any story that is worthy of the name will find a ready market, regardless of the viewpoint from which it is written.

The viewpoint from which a story should be written is a matter that only the author can decide for himself. He should size up his story-idea and then select the angle of narration which, in his opinion, will permit him to unfold his plot with the greatest effect and make the most of the various situations with which he will have to deal. But whatever the viewpoint, once it has been selected, the writer should stick to it with the tenacity of a bulldog. If he yields to the impulse to shift to another angle when it comes, as it surely will come sooner or later, he will find himself the author of one of those two-or-more-stories-in-one monstrosities that rouse the ire of our friends the editors.

The tendency to shift the angle of narration, which is especially strong in the beginner, may be traced to several causes: First, because the original viewpoint does not live up to its promise, and the author is forced to shift to another viewpoint in order to unfold his plot; second, because the author deliberately plans the shift, believing that, from the standpoint of effect, his story will be the gainer if presented from two or more angles of narration; and third, because the writer is lazy or lax in his methods and is content to get his story down on paper, with little regard for the manner in which it is written.

Present-day writers certainly have a multitude of bad examples to call up in defense of the tendency to shift the viewpoint, for it was just as prevalent among authors of past generations as it is among those of today.

In "Treasure Island" Stevenson shifts from the viewpoint of Jim Hawkins, from whose angle most of the story is told, to that of the Doctor. After a few chapters he shifts back to the original viewpoint. In "Bleak House" there is a similar shift when Dickens switches from the author's viewpoint to that of Esther Summerson. In "The Golden Scorpion," to which attention has already been directed, Rohmer makes a similar shift, with more success than some of his predecessors; but there is no doubt but that this novel, as well as all other novels in which there is a break in the angle of narration, would have been more effective if the author had stuck to a single viewpoint.

A shift of viewpoints in a short-story is usually even more awkward than it is in a novel. Even Kipling and Doyle failed to carry it off with success, as many of their stories bear evidence. Turning to the work of more recent writers, 'orrible examples can be found in almost any magazine. "The Keys of Ausable," a story published in Red Book, is written from the viewpoint of Jimmy Hazelton, but in the very middle of the story the author, Edward Mott Woolley, switches to another viewpoint to write of a single episode. In this case, the fault is not a very serious one, for Woolley wields "a wicked pen"; but the story would have been the gainer had it been written from a single viewpoint.

In "Savagery," a *Harper's* story, by Charles Nordhoff, is found a typical story-within-a-story. Nordhoff, writing in the first person, opens the story with a description of old Jackson; then follow a sketch of mountains that lean against the sea in the moonlight, a bit of ancient history, a few philosophical reflections, and a rambling account of a character who proves to be the inciting motive of the story. Then the author leans back in his chair and lets Jackson tell the story in his own way.

A somewhat similar situation is found in the "Wolfville" stories by Alfred Henry Lewis. The stories proper are told in the first person by the Old Cattleman, but the author occasionally shifts the viewpoint long enough to throw in a useless comment while the narrator "lights a cigar" or "calls for a drink of nose-paint." The Wolfville stories are good stories, and they are not greatly injured by these lapses. Nevertheless, they are unnecessary and might well have been dispensed with.

There is one other fault in this connection to which attention should be directed, for while it is not as common now as it was fifty years ago, it is occasionally found in the work of the genial tyro and the self-esteemed professional. I have reference to the habit some authors have of intruding themselves into their stories. After a hearty dinner and half-a-dozen bottles of wine Dumas could seldom resist the temptation to speak in parenthetical asides to his "dear readers." The fault is a common one with the old French and English writers, and is also found in the work of Ivan Turgenev, the Russian writer. Much can be forgiven genius, but there is no legitimate excuse for an author's becoming personal in a story written in the third person. It annoys the reader, and therefore should be avoided.

It might well be asked why editors buy stories of the story-within-a-story variety if they are looked upon with such disfavor. The answer is that editors, like all other human beings, cannot always get what they want. It has been estimated that there are over a hundred thousand people in the United States alone who buck the writing game with more or less regularity, but only a very small percentage of them turn out a steady flow of salable material. There are never enough high-class stories to meet the demand, and editors are sometimes forced to purchase manuscripts in spite of technical faults that they feel the ordinary reader may sense but not always detect.

Whether or not there is ever justification for a shift of viewpoint is a question upon which writers and most editors, I think, will agree. That such a practice confuses the reader, however, there can be no doubt. A break in the angle of narration derails the reader's train of thought and distracts his interest from the main issue. There is no pleasure in being switched off from time to time into a number of by-roads; the reader wants to follow the main line of the story through from the beginning to the end.

There may be trick plots that call for such an innovation, but such plots are the exception rather than the rule, and they are not of the kind that would be looked upon by the average editor with favor.

The writer who wishes to sell his stories—and who of us does not?—should stick to the approved methods. Select your angle of narration and grimly pursue it to the end. If you find that the viewpoint you have adopted does not live up to your expectations, tear up the manuscript and bravely attack the story from a different angle. But this will seldom if ever be necessary if you will give the matter the consideration that is its due before you begin the actual writing of a story. A story should be carefully mapped out in the writer's mind before it is set down on paper, and when this rule is adhered to, the viewpoint from which the story is to be written is usually a matter of natural selection. And when this occurs you can put your pen to paper with little fear of making a false start.

Chunn has a pretty black and white view when it comes to changing the point of view mid-story, and with good reason. Every time you jump viewpoints, the reader has to do some extra work to get back into the story. And as to the "frame" story, when a character sets up and tells the real story- I can only think of one time where it added something important to the story.

Of course, accidental and unintentional viewpoint switching should be edited out. I've read a few in the slush pile that switched back and forth between first person and third person mid scene. It is extremely jarring.

WHY I DECLINE STORIES

By Sonya Levien
From the November, 1921 issue of *The Writer's Monthly*
Fiction Editor of *The Metropolitan* Magazine

In choosing fiction for a popular magazine one must be sure first of all that the story will appeal to a large audience of readers. It must have the essential quality of holding the attention. A story which the editor has to make an effort to read is not very likely to receive much attention from anyone else. On the other hand, if a story, through the qualities of form, construction, style, and the needed element of suspense, literally carries one along from page to page, it has at least the first essential quality of a popular magazine-story.

Aside from the actual merit of a story there are so many varied considerations that enter into its acceptance or rejection that one cannot with justice put down a definite set of rules for an author to follow. There are the questions of the character of the material already on hand, of editorial policy, of the make-up facilities of a particular magazine— considerations that the author knows nothing of. For reasons of this sort a story turned down by a lesser magazine is sometimes snapped up by a magazine of higher literary standards. And yet this circumstance does not indicate that the first editor is a blind hack or prove the author to be an unappreciated genius—though often the author imagines this to be the case.

When you apply yourself to the task of selecting a very small percentage of the thousands of manuscripts that come in during a year, you do consciously or unconsciously evolve a set of rules by which the final verdict of Yes or No is governed. And the usual reasons for the *No's* constitute the set of warnings to authors I would like to enumerate herewith.

To put the matter simply, editors buy the stories they believe will interest their audience; they return those stories that fail in that purpose. But in truth we are only working on a hypothesis, for our audience is the silent multitude: composed of those who read silently, judge silently, and act silently, by refusing to buy the magazine if they do not enjoy its contents, by buying it if they do. Seldom do they give us their opinion in any other way. It would be easier for us if we could see them clap their hands, hear their hurrahs or their hisses, and thereby know where we have won out or failed. Like the blind, we must surmise the temper of our audience by intuition, by intelligence, if we can.

So uncertain is the result that some editors, in order to play safe, will stick to what they consider sure bets, and only buy the work of authors who are known to produce best sellers. But that is not always a paying proposition for either the editor or the author. In such cases the editor has to pay a uniformly high price for all the author's work, and no author can keep up an equal standard of popularity; and when the attempt is made, it often leads to failure and a loss of the very quality sought. We of the Metropolitan maintain that this is a poor, makeshift way of creating a magazine. It may result in a brilliant array of names, but it is certain to produce a monotonous effect in the long run. No author does his best work on a strictly trade and commission basis.

To learn what will please the multitude and how to discover it constitutes the real problem of the editor. Once I thought I was on the brink of knowing the secret. I found myself during the six o'clock rush hour on a crowded elevated train squeezed up against two girls who were discussing "The Rosary," Mrs. Barclay's novel that sold over a million copies in this country. From their talk I surmised that these two girls were insatiable consumers of fiction. One of them was relating the story of "The Rosary" and ended up with "It's a grand story, I tell you! It makes you feel—it makes you feel. . . ." Just then the train guard called their station. I was young enough at that time to believe in the open sesame panaceas and millenniums, and though it was not my station I rushed out and followed after them. When I was about a mile out of my way, I heard the final words, which were, "Well, Lizzie, that story just gets you!"

And yet, in that inarticulate way of hers, Lizzie's friend, to use her own way of putting it, "hit the nail on the head." We usually find that when a story "gets us," it is apt to get somebody else.

Therefore the first test of a short-story is whether or not it compels the attention. One can reverse the argument by saying that those stories which do not hold the attention are returned. And it is not as bigoted and narrow a test as it sounds. As a normal person, of catholic taste, an editor who finds himself aroused and stirred by a story stands a better chance of pleasing his audience with that story than if he were constantly trying to guess at the tastes of a vague and inarticulate mass of subscribers.

During the years I have read and returned stories I find that many rejected manuscripts fall into certain types. I am not speaking of those stories that are too poor to be considered, but of that large number of stories that have enough merit to go the rounds and find a place for themselves eventually—the story that is often returned to the discouraged author with an encouraging letter.

THE SLIGHT STORY

A large number of rejected stories fall under the head of Slight—a story that is just fairly told, and whose incidents are so put together that the effect on the whole does not move one vitally.

Now there is a type of author whose success does not depend upon the choice of an important theme because he says whatever he wants to with so much charm and humor that it does not matter in the long run about what he writes. A good example is Irving Cobb. He writes as many a woman knits—line by line, without close concentration on the form the garment will eventually take. Such an author depends largely for effect upon the style or manner of delivery. If he has natural humor, he is fortunate in his creation. If to his humor is added a depth of conception, a love for humanity, he is bound to be of the beloved. When his discursiveness unearths the humor and pathos of everyday life, he becomes the most popular of authors, like Finley Peter Dunne and Mark Twain. Their material does not have to have plots; it has wit and humor, understanding, charm and style.

But in most cases, when the writing "comes easy" and there is not important substance in the story, the author runs the great danger of wordiness and overwrites himself. Thus if an author has no faculty for humor, or for style, then he must be careful to provide for himself plenty of substance and to write about something that will stir his readers.

It is perhaps somewhat the same with magazine editors as with other persons, such as painters and musicians, who manifest their tastes more directly—we go in for very different degrees of intensity in the portrayal of life. I can think of editors who pin their faith, because they like it, to clever, thin, pale specimens of the art of fiction; of others who love the middle register of common life; and still others who go in for the heights and depths of emotion, the passionate crises which after all do enter into the lives of practically all people. There are many ways of interesting the public; but the author who cannot depend for effect on style or humor had best go in for dynamic fiction. A story must be more than a mere mess of pretty words.

An author who has at least reached the stage of—I do not say popularity—but a place where his publishers have sufficient faith in his drawing power to get his short stories out in book form, used to send me the type of story we are talking about—lots of style and no substance. His style was charming; he wrote with imagination and flexibility—the flexibility, the wordiness of Henry James—but usually the story was about a spring hat or the color of a cat's tail, so to speak. One day at a dinner party in a Boston house he accused me of always praising his stories and yet turning them down. I told him that H. G. Wells had once said of Henry James' work that his writings were like a colossal cathedral, intricately carved; that the altar was artistic and beautiful; on the altar stood a plate of gold; and on the plate lay a dead rabbit. Not that I agree with Wells, for I am a faithful follower of Henry James, but it was a vivid illustration of what I meant by lack of substance. We went on to discuss what constituted substance. I told my friend that with his style and charm of expression, if he chose themes that had vitality, he would find a ready market for his work. And then and there we began to hunt for dynamic themes. I remember both of us getting so excited over the conversation that we were unaware that the other guests had stopped eating and were listening to us, while we were tearing out such expressions as murder, jealousy, hate, love, divorce, abduction.

And now when he sends me a story of his he always says, "I hope that you will find that this manuscript contains enough of Love, Murder, Hate, Jealousy, etc." He still knits, but knits with a pattern.

THE SHOP-TALK STORY

Another type of short story we invariably have to return let us call the shop-talk story—the story with which the reporter tries to break into the magazine, the story of how the young hero reporter, who, just as he was about to be bounced, comes in at the eleventh hour with a scoop and saves the paper, and then marries the young lady space-writer. A variation of even feebler appeal is the newspaper story that is written around a few literary characters—the mere highbrow story.

Although a writer can describe more realistically the kind of life he knows, the emotions he feels, etc., etc., yet if the details and emotions are too closely personal to him they may move other reporters but will not touch outside readers, men and women who have never been inside a newspaper office and who are not to be stirred beyond endurance by the word "scoop." Stories aimed at popular magazines must have a wide appeal. There lies to my thinking the difference in the popularity of "Main Street" and "Moon Calf." Main Streeters all over the United States feel that they have a hand in the Main Street pie, whereas "Moon Calf," though a better constructed piece of work, is, as I heard one reader say, "another couple of hundred thousand words about a queer writing-fellow and his problems."

I do not mean to say that we never accept newspaper stories. We are glad to get them when the plot is one that is able to stir those outside the writing profession.

THE PROPAGANDUM STORY

Another type of story that usually finds its way back is the propagandum story. We consider that the American public takes its work seriously. If you feel that you must preach to it, give it a tract. In the magazine we tell our readers, in our articles, that they are slackers in one thing or another and try to bring them up to an ideal level of civic responsibility; therefore we feel doubly that in our fiction they are entitled to pure entertainment. Fiction is no doubt the greatest factor in the moulding of public opinion, but the author should never aim directly at this result. The influence of his story must be felt indirectly, as in consequence of the moral feeling created by the narrative.

There never must be any preaching at the reader. Feminist propagandum creeps in most often. There are some authors, mostly young ones, who think that they take a direct road to fame when they choose for their theme the subject of illegitimacy. They expect that their courage in writing sympathetically about illicit passion will put their product in the literary class. Usually I get a letter with such a story saying, "I am afraid you won't be brave enough to print this"—or, with more obvious salesmanship—"Yours is the only magazine brave enough to print this." Such a theme may denote a broadmindedness toward social and ethical questions, but the story, merely by its choice of theme, does not thereby become a masterpiece. I replied to a young friend who sent me such a letter with his manuscript that with editors illegitimacy was not sufficient in itself, but had to be made interesting before it induced acceptance.

And that brings us to a discussion of what are the relative chances of the so-called immoral stories, and stories with "sad endings," etc. Let us consider first the immoral story.

Recently we printed a narrative about two shop girls. One, a weak sister, had an illegitimate baby—the friend, the strong one, adopted it and brought it up as her own illegitimate child. After great travail the story ended happily. We found the manuscript interesting and realistic. We printed it though we knew that a certain percentage of our readers would object. We were absolutely right in gauging the result. We had several vehement, bitter letters stating that the story was immoral, that the immoral girl should not have come out unpunished. Several people said that the magazine could no longer come into the house.

In accepting the story we took into consideration the high degree of its interests, its suspense, and also its literary style. In order to justify the theme we demanded a higher degree of these three qualities than usual. It had to be exceptionally well written and gripping in order to counteract the obvious criticism of the more conventional portion of our readers. In short, the story with illegitimacy for its theme must be an artistic production.

THE STORY WITH A SAD ENDING

A similar fate of judgment awaits the story with a sad ending—it must have greater compensation in other respects in order to overcome the handicap of its sad ending. Some of you may argue with justice against such a decision. You will say that life is not all love and honey. True. But when a human being seems to be "down and out" there will usually be found some spark of hope in him. When the author does for his hero and heroine in the last paragraph, he leaves no hope behind. Moreover, it is our general aim to offer readers stories that will give them enjoyable relaxation and not those that will depress them and make them unhappy.

For the same reason there exists in many editorial offices a prejudice against morbid, depressing and unwholesome stories—stories that chiefly depend for holding the attention and for excitement upon crime, cruelty and sordidness. Editors feel that their prejudice represents the natural antagonism of the healthy person against the point of view that does not go with wholesome and buoyant living. Also, the great majority of readers demand romance in fiction, perhaps to counteract the prosaic reality of their existence. And since it is our purpose to cater to the majority we prefer stories that have happy endings.

The Unconvincing Story

The greatest number of stories to be turned down are the unconvincing stories. Often when I return a manuscript with the criticism that it is unconvincing, the author writes back and says, "But it is a true story." So much the worse for the author. A story is unconvincing because the author has not the art to call forth the emotion necessary to make you believe that the events which he says happened really did happen. The author must not forget that the readers are not participants in the events that he is describing; they are merely willing onlookers, and if he wants them to sympathize, to shed tears with the characters, he must make them feel emotionally, in their own persons, the suspense and strain that the characters in reality would feel. If an author is writing about a murder he must remember to create a murder for his readers. Through his imagination his words must portray the deep hate of the one who committed the murder and he must make the reader suffer the bereavement, the agonizing loss to the circle of the murdered person's beloved ones. If the author fails in one iota to create the emotions these characters would have suffered in real life, his readers know that he is begging at the door of reality and only writing fiction. To make a story convincing you must feel emotionally, through the creative imagination, the depths of feeling you are making your characters undergo. The plot must ring true, and the characters must be so vividly and honestly created that the reader will accept them as the exact prototypes of living beings.

THE STORY WITH A FOREIGN SETTING

The story with the foreign setting, particularly with a Chinese setting, is having a vogue just now owing to the success of "Limehouse Nights." But authors must remember that they cannot treat the simple everyday habits of foreigners and expect American readers to respond with sympathy and interest. For instance, it is difficult for American readers to feel like beating their chests with anguish because a Japanese son says to his father,"You're an old fool!" A Japanese no doubt would be "knocked down" by such a beginning, but in America it is too ordinary an occurrence to have children utter candid opinions about their parents, to have any effect. The usual run of Chinese and Japanese stories we receive, about a son who sacrificed his life for an doddering old idiot of a father, never draw a tear.

The author who wants to write stories about foreign countries for an American audience must remember to choose dramatic episodes. The plot must be a thriller, the setting colorful and vivid. The story must appeal to the imagination of the audience as well as to the emotion. The illusion and the glamour of the foreign setting should be kept up throughout and are of primary importance. Burke does this in "Limehouse Nights." Every sentence in his short-stories—and they are very short—creates a vivid picture, colorful, strong, thrilling, that cannot but appeal as romantic to office-ridden Americans.

~

I have here tried to give a general survey of the various types of stories most often rejected, but I should like to take this opportunity to say in all earnestness that an editor's job is not to find reasons for rejecting stories but to find stories to accept. When we come across an unusual, creative piece of writing that we can use in the magazine, the day is made. I have written letters of acceptance that have thrilled me with as much pleasure as the authors could possibly have felt when they received them. And when I have found a good story and know that it is the kind that will please and stir a great many readers, I feel that I share in the joy of the creator of it, by being a link in the chain that places it before the public.

I do not hold with many of the teachers of the short story that young writers should follow the magazines implicitly, and learn their trade therefrom. The life of a magazine fiction reader is made sufficiently dull and depressing by the sameness of manuscripts received from established authors. That is why I always put my tongue in my cheek when some author says that editors don't recognize the unusual. If this ever happens it is because the sameness of nine-tenths of the material has reduced him or her to a state of insensibility. It is my belief that the beginner should learn from the best there is in literature and keep in mind a standard created by great talent rather than that of successful hacks. Read magazines to study the market, but *never for the purpose of imitation.* It is the best art that wins in the long run, and the least originality stands a better chance of success than clever imitative work where the author makes an obvious play to the gallery. It is my opinion that American authorship is too easily encouraged to think itself great and finished. Perhaps this is because we judge too much by the dollar standard. The author who is paid more is often erroneously considered the greater writer. And yet this very false standard is the undoing of the overpaid author. For the temptation to write for money is great and the author usually ends by producing monotonous, mechanical stuff. When the writer measures his success solely by the dollar sign, it is then that success is most apt to leave him. Thus the undesirable circle completes itself.

To the new author I would say: "Be brave, be brave at all costs." I do not mean be brave in the selection of the theme about which you want to write, but in those subtle honesties of characterization and motive that lie behind the written words in every story. Do not be in the least afraid of putting yourself frankly into your work. The editor will be much more interested by the freshness and vitality you put into the story than by the conventional devices of short story writing.

If you want to write your story in the first person, do so. If you want to use one-syllable words and two-word sentences, do so. Don't feel that because the best story of the year began with an introduction, yours must have one. Get the greatest possible enjoyment of self-expression you can out of your idea by following your own instincts in your own creation. We are always more delighted with a story that, although crudely written, has newness and vitality than with a conventional, machine-made manuscript, no matter how well the latter is put together.

Here are the primary reasons Levien states that she rejects stories:
1. *The story does not grab and hold attention.*
2. *The story does not engage the reader's emotions.*
3. *The story has too narrow appeal.*
4. *The story is thinly-veiled propaganda.*
5. *The story has a dismal ending.*
6. *The story does not elicit enough emotion to feel real.*
7. *The story misuses a foreign setting.*

How to Write Description Without Slowing the Story

By Frank Bennett

From the *1958 Writer's Yearbook*

The simplest sentence, "I saw a house.", creates a picture. The weakness of this picture is that it doesn't look the same to everyone who reads it. In my mind is a small, frame house. In reading it, you may picture a large brick house. By adding two words, "small, frame", I could have given you a clearer picture. As I see it, this is the author's obligation to his reader: present the reader with as clear a picture as words will permit, doing so in as painless, unobtrusive and interesting a manner as possible.

To the beginning writer casually reading today's magazine fiction, it may seem that the description of locales and settings is hardly worthy of consideration because it seems to occupy so little space in a story. The truth of the matter is, description has as important a part in a story's effectiveness today as it did in the unrushed days of the past. The writer of today's magazine fiction weaves his description, or "word pictures", so neatly into the other business of the story that it is sometimes difficult to isolate it as description. But it is there — a word here, a phrase there — and, done as it should be, it makes its impact upon the reader without his realizing how or why. Today's story-telling technique is to keep description from intruding on the forward movement of the story.

As an example of this interweaving of description, I quote from one of my own stories which appeared in a recent issue of *Family Circle* — "The Beautiful Destroyer" :

His father met him at the front gate. "Are you equal to a ride in the car?" he asked Jule.

"Sure," Jule answered.

"Let's go, then," his father said.

Even before his father made the first turn, Jule guessed they were going to Lookout Hill. In the clearing at the top of the hill, his father halted the car, and they sat in silence, looking out on the great checkerboard of farms and timberlands, green and brown and golden.

"Son," his father said, breaking the hush, "I've always planned to give you this west half section..."

Notice how the descriptions are mingled with the business of movement, all working together to give effectiveness to the scene. You travel from the front gate to Lookout Hill without any words wasted in telling you that Jule and his father climbed into the car, started it, and drove along the crooked road that led to the top of the hill. You know the hill is in a wooded region, because the car was halted in a clearing. You know it must be the highest hill in the region — the very name tells you that, plus the checkerboard effect of the fields below. They sit in silence — therefore they must be awed by the beauty and grandeur of the scene. It is a quiet, isolated place, for when the father speaks, he breaks the hush. Through the setting of this stage — in which the father gives land to his son — the story line moves forward, for you are seeing the picture through the character's own feelings and reactions.

Long, descriptive passages arc no longer necessary in fiction. Except for some extremely unusual scene they have lost their original functional reason for being. The modern reader, through movies, television, photography and travel, has seen practically everything there is to see. So for the magazine reader a word or two can many times set the stage of a scene, whereas a generation back, a paragraph or a page would be needed. To illustrate: "John walked into the isolation booth."

"Isolation booth" sets the stage, for what modern reader hasn't at one time or another seen the famed isolation booth on television? But if you had had John walk into the booth fifteen years ago (should there have been such a contraption), a great deal of explaining and describing would have been necessary.

In today's fiction, the stage upon which the characters perform is set not in big doses that halt the forward march of the story, but in small doses that fit into the action so smoothly that the reader is scarcely aware of them as description. He simply forms his mental pictures of the stage properties *as he follows* the story line. These mental images give him something solid to hold on to. They make for a feeling of reality. They make the actions of the characters seem plausible. And they add to the entertainment and informative value of a story. The average reader thinks in terms of pictures. Take away his pictures, and you have taken away all.

Here are a few of the methods by which today's authors infuse descriptive matter into their work.

Statement of facts by the author. As an example, from Steve McNeil's *Post* story, "The Girl Who Took Sun Baths":

> To the left of the office were a number of small hangars housing aircraft, partially owned by Country Airways, Inc., partially owned by various banks. There were two crop-dusting airplanes which had had their power thoughtfully doubled, four small trainers, a helicopter and a four-place job with retractable gear, butterfly tail, a full panel and plush upholstery. This airplane was used mainly for charter.

Mr. McNeil is a master at giving the reader a solid block of description and making him like it. He does this with conversational asides such as "partially owned by various banks" and "their power thoughtfully doubled." Until a beginner acquires this skill, he does well to steer away from paragraphs of description by statement of facts.

Setting the stage through its effect on the character's senses. This is quite effective, for every reader, from the time of birth until the day he reads your story, has learned about his own world through the senses of sight, sound, touch, taste and smell, and he can understand and picture the world you have created for him if you give it to him through the five senses. I quote from my *Redbook* novel, "So Brief a Spring":

Now Mike was speaking, saying something about the shabby buildings and poorly lighted streets, but Lily wasn't listening. She was hearing the clanking of freight engines, the rumbling of mills, the bawling of frightened cattle. She was smelling the dust, the coal smoke, the stench.

Description woven in with an emotional effect on the characters. As an example, from Alice Lent Covert's *Post* story, "Moment of Fear":

> The fear came first, the cold and painful hollowness inside Corby, the shameful trembling of his hands. Outside, the steel disk that was the January sun sank, its last half-hearted rays touching the polished silver skin of the B-47 boring through the thin, still air thirty-five thousand feet above the North Atlantic.
>
> Corby glanced up. Some trick of the dying sunlight silvered the plastic canopy, making briefly of it a dim mirror, so that he saw himself as a vague, masked figure. "Lieutenant Corby, sir," he thought bitterly, "the frightened Lieutenant John King Corby."

The above method is favored by today's slick writers.

Description given through the memories of a character. From my *Redbook* story, "A Tree in Bloom":

> Then he takes off to look around a bit, leaving me alone with the tree. As I sit drinking in its beauty, it seems to me that I am a child once again, playing under the redbud in my mother's tiny back yard with its soft carpet of grass, the green wooden bench and a white lattice fence.

Another method of setting the stage is *through a character's dialogue.* This example from my *Farm Journal* story, titled "Ride into the Unknown". In this an old-timer is spinning a tall tale:

> "That stagecoach was a whingdinger. All white, with gleaming gold lamps, and wheels with heavy tires that looked like solid

silver. And them six white horses hitched to it – say, you boys never saw nothing like them horses! Gold rings on their harness. Their hides brushed until it hurt your eyes to look at 'em."

Your job as a writer is to present your make-believe world so vividly that your reader, if he should be reading in the middle of the day about something that is happening at night, will be astonished when he lifts his eyes to see that the sun is shining. In setting the stage with word pictures, one must bear this in mind: if a scene is not real and clear-cut in the author's mind, it cannot be real to the reader.

For example, a tree has many qualities that appeal to the senses. These could be put in words as follows: gentle whispering of the leaves, sighing of the wind through the branches, deep cool shade, a skeleton against a cold winter sky, etc. In your descriptive passage, give the quality that is most effective for the scene. For example : "deep cool shade" could be most effective in a scene in which the hero halts his tiresome journey on a hot clay.

Allow the reader a yardstick for comparisons. For example, if you've established that your hero is a tall, agile man. and now you want your reader to form some notion of the distance between a window and a door: "John turned from the window and crossed to the door in three quick strides." Remember, the reader doesn't want to take time out to think in terms of feet and inches; he wants information to come to him in terms of action or emotion.

Careful observation on the author's part of the world about him affords a basis upon which to create the effective background for his characters' performances. Once imagined, show the scene through your own individuality as a writer. Be concerned with the authenticity of details. Build your scene of things within the reader's experiences.

To give a scene reality, pick out some small detail and present it sharply against the whole, as: "He came to a line fence that stretched across the prairie as far as the eye could see. For a moment, a tuft of white wool that clung to a rusty bent barb caught his attention."

In closing, I have this suggestion: go on from where I have left off in this brief article by doing some thoughtful study of the magazines for which you hope to write. Daily practice helps a lot.

I really like that little bit of advice near the end - describe the whole by contrasting with a small detail. Of course, the starting advice holds true today - don't stop the narration to take a long description break. Unless you are an epic fantasy writer with a horde of adoring fans, your readers will get bored and walk away.

The Poorest Excuse

By Magda Leigh
Originally published in the December, 1923 issue of *The Editor*

The poorest excuse for not accomplishing anything is the excuse of lack of time. People who claim that they want to write, more than anything else on earth, disprove their statements by using this excuse. Almost invariably one can make time, even if one cannot find it.

Many people also claim that they do not write because of lack of place to work. They feel that they must have offices fitted up with all literary devices, that otherwise they cannot be "inspired." Our own conviction is that one can write wherever one has elbow-space and determination.

The trouble with most of us is that we are mentally indolent. We dream. We like to picture ourselves as writers; we read about other writers. But when it comes to the actual labor of writing, we find a half dozen reasons for not doing it.

Theodore Roosevelt found time to write. Yet we know of no time in his mature years when he was not an extraordinarily busy man. His brain was always alert and constructive.

Mary Roberts Rinehart is a good example of the woman writer who has found time to become a successful author as well as a successful wife and mother. In spite of her literary career, she has never neglected her family, and takes pride in emphasizing this fact.

Rupert Hughes, known among his associates as "the human dynamo," finds time to write short stories, novels, photoplay continuities, and to direct some of his own pictures. He seldom refuses to meet people who come to the studio to see him, and he seems never too busy not to have time to take an interest in a young writer.

The trouble is that although many of us declare we wish to write, we actually don't wish to write so much as we wish to be known as writers! It seems to tickle one's ego to be pointed out as an author. So much so, in fact, that it looks as if authorship were the most enviable of all professions or arts or businesses.

There is little excuse for us not to write, if we wish to. A trifle earlier rising hour, or a slightly later bed-time, or some squeezing together of odd moments during the day, and the time is made.

As for having no place to write, one needs no place save a seat to sit upon and room for one's elbow. Morgan Robertson, in his days of poverty, used for a desk a board placed across the sink or tub in the kitchen.

Ethelda Hesser, of The Editor Family, whose first novel, "Inner Darkness," is to be published by Harper's, has told us how she wrote her book: "on a board in my lap, and standing up at the piano, and at the kitchen table, because my desk was upstairs and it was too hot up there to think."

The real reason for not writing, of course, is that some of us find, after we have made a start, that writing is not as easy, in closeup, as in a long-shot view! We are not zealots enough to make any sacrifice for our ambition. If thoughts do not flow easily, we find that loophole of excuse: no time.

Too, many of us make a start, meet with a little discouragement, and immediately find a dozen excuses to discontinue.

It is folly to try to map out any routine to suit the requirements of many authors. Each must find his own way. One writer may work best at night; another finds his brain clearest in the early hours of the morning.

At this particular season of the year, the magazines are buying rather freely. It is a poor season in which to be a slacker. Summer is the best time to "lack time," for the market is dull during vacation months.

Sporadic writing never gets anyone anywhere. The man who arrives is the man who continually drills forward. He does not complain of lack of time and opportunity. He makes both, by hook or by crook. But then, this man is a Writer, not a dreamer.

We scarcely know how to stimulate the lagging interest of these people who can't find time! As a matter of fact, their stimulation should come from an inner fire. There should be such an urge to write that nothing can prevent progress. This inner fire, this compelling urge, this driving force —these are the things that signify at least a spark of ability. Where they don't exist, we doubt if any real ability exists. Writing is not something one forces oneself to, but something that drives one before it like a whole gale, at sea.

Indeed, the real writer, whose heart is full of his work, has to find time for his other duties, since his writing comes first. The trouble with the literary slackers is that their hearts have not been touched. Authorship just appeals to their minds, thus far, and therefore they do not get beyond thinking and talking about it!

No, if writing does not sweep over you like a tide and carry you along with it, make up your mind that authorship is scarcely for you. Write, if you must, for your own amusement, but don't try to write professionally. The field is full of men and women who care so vitally about authorship that they devote the better part of their lives to it, studying, working, polishing what they have done, struggling for betterment, enduring discouragements—almost starving for the achievement of their ambition.

These people find time. Writing is the breath of life to them. Whether they make their mark—whether their marks be little or big—at least they have proven their sincerity by writing.

Thousands of people are keeping physically fit by their daily dozen. A mental daily dozen of some kind or other would be of benefit to the writer. It would form the habit of finding time, and would probably grow because of its own worth.

It's even easier to find ways to write now than when this was written. There are a good number of authors who write whole novels with their thumbs whenever they can squeeze it in. There are word processors on every device you can carry around. You can do it anywhere, anytime. I can't wait to read your masterpiece.

Thank You for Reading

Thanks for reading. If you enjoyed this book, please consider leaving a review wherever you bought it.

Thanks,

Bryce Beattie

vintagewritinginstruction.com